THE
DISCIPLESHIP

THE WAY OF DISCIPLESHIP

MARK 8 TO 10 / GRAHAM TWELFTREE

AN ALBATROSS BOOK

© Commentary: Graham Twelftree 1993
© Discussion questions: Albatross Books Pty Ltd 1993

Published in Australia and New Zealand by
Albatross Books Pty Ltd
PO Box 320, Sutherland
NSW 2232, Australia
in the United States of America by
Albatross Books
PO Box 131, Claremont
CA 91711, USA
and in the United Kingdom by
The Bible Reading Fellowship
Peter's Way, Sandy Lane West
Oxford OX4 5HG, England

First edition 1993

National Library of Australia
Cataloguing-in-Publication data

Twelftree, Graham
The Way of Discipleship

ISBN 0   86760 146 9 (Albatross)
ISBN 0   7459 2183 3 (BRF)

1. Bible. N.T. Mark – Criticism, interpretation, etc.
I. Title

226.306

Cover photo: John Graham
Printed and bound in Australia by Griffin Paperbacks, Netley, SA

Contents

Foreword

IT IS ONE THING TO become a follower of Jesus. It is quite another thing to go on living as one of his followers.

Mark is a book of the New Testament I read often, for it reminds me of the purpose of being a follower of Jesus, and how to remain faithful to him while living with my failures, the demands of others and his demand for total obedience.

Mark is also a special book for me because it takes seriously the suffering involved in being a follower of Jesus and it encourages me to take up the challenge of living sacrificially, not losing sight of the unseen glory God has for us in the future. The aim of this book is to make clear what Mark is telling us about being a follower of Jesus.

My prayer is, with Saint Augustine: 'Lord, whatever I have said in this book that comes from your prompting, may your people recognise it; for what I have said that comes only from myself, I ask forgiveness from you and your people.'[1]

Graham Twelftree
March 1993

Introduction

The story so far

IN THE MOVIE 'THE MISSION', a priest climbs mountains and confronts obstacles to take the good news of Jesus to people who murdered a member of his order. In Nepal, a follower of Jesus is threatened by local villagers that, if he gives his daughter a Christian funeral, he will be charged with murdering his daughter; he goes ahead with the funeral and is now in custody awaiting trial for murder. In Australia, a Christian loses his job because he refuses to enter into a dishonest business deal.

What does it mean to be a follower of Jesus? What sort of people are Christians supposed to be and how are they supposed to live as modern disciples of Jesus? More importantly, where can they find out what it means to be disciples?

One of the best places to look is in the middle section of Mark's Gospel — chapter 8, verse 22 to chapter 10, verse 52.

It seems surprising that Mark was once a neglected book. Despite early popularity, it was relegated to centuries of virtual obscurity because Augustine thought that Mark was merely an abbreviation of Matthew. For the last 150 years, however, since the establishment of the view that Mark was the first Gospel to be written, this fascinating book has enjoyed increasing attention.

The Gospel has even been taken up by the actor Alec McCowen and recited on the stage in London and New York to the delight of audience and critic alike. Being a 'masterpiece of amazing originality', as someone put it recently, Mark presents us with all kinds of interesting questions and problems and has been the subject of a multitude of interesting theories.

However, it is in dealing with the identity and purpose of Jesus and focussing on the issue of what it means to be a follower of Jesus that Mark's story remains of unparalleled importance to Christians of any time, including our own.

Who, when, where and why?
❏ *Who wrote the Gospel?*
The title, 'The Gospel According to Mark', was most probably in place by the second century. As Greek writers in this period no longer published their works anonymously, it is quite possible that this

Gospel is to be associated in some way with Mark. Tradition has generally identified the author with the Mark or John Mark (probably the same person) found elsewhere in the New Testament.[1] Although some have seen an autobiographical note in the mention of a young man fleeing naked from the scene of Jesus' arrest,[2] few scholars support this view for, if it were a personal reminiscence, it would fit better with the previous story.

So we cannot be sure who wrote this little book. Those who were first acquainted with the contents of it probably heard it read to them in one of their gatherings. Perhaps they already knew the writer or, in view of the significance of what they were hearing, it did not matter to them. Indeed, the reversal of the customary title so that the supposed author's name is last in the title bears out this view that the message was and is the important issue, not the identity of the writer.

❏ *When and where was it written?*

Irenaeus, bishop of Lyons towards the end of the second century, implies that, at the earliest, Mark was written in Rome during the persecution of Nero in AD 64.[3] Further, unlike Matthew and Luke who used Mark as a source and wrote after the destruction of the Temple in Jerusalem in AD 70, Mark is not coloured by the event.[4]

In view of the frankness with which Peter is depicted, which would make most sense after his martyrdom in the persecutions of Nero in AD 64, it is probable that Mark was written between this date and the fall of the Temple. The year AD 69 is a particularly likely date. It was a fearful year in Rome[5] and the backdrop of the Gospel is one of discipleship under pressure; also, as the author was expecting to see the Antichrist in the Temple,[6] the book is likely to have been published that year in Rome.

❏ *Why was the Gospel written?*
If we know why Mark wrote his Gospel, it will help us understand his message for our time.

It is generally agreed that, prior to the publication of Mark, the stories of Jesus were only circulating by word of mouth and had not been collected together to make a continuous story. Why did Mark choose to bring together individual stories, collections of stories and summaries of Jesus' ministry — as well as material about Jesus' suffering and death — to construct his Gospel?

As we will see through the remainder of this study, a key issue for Mark was the identity of Jesus and the precise nature of his ministry. But for whom did Mark think this was an issue: Christians or non-Christians? It seems reasonable to conclude that Mark did not tell his story of Jesus and his first followers as a tract for the evangelisation of the masses. Rather, he was most probably writing to people who were already Christians.

The issues or points of tension in the story — the question about fasting, the use of the sabbath, ceremonial defilement, the ambition of James and John to sit next to Jesus in glory[7] — would be of little interest to the non-Christian. Similarly, the teaching Mark gives on divorce and forgiveness, and the stories on exorcism, humility and on trust and prayer[8] are directed to the teaching of Christians.

Even the stories of the call of the first disciples[9] seem to be included for the encouragement of the existing followers of Jesus, rather than to win outsiders as new followers, for this material is dominated by the invitation to be involved in mission.

Also, the call to persevere in discipleship and the acknowledged possibility of apostasy show us that Mark is writing to Christians to encourage them not to be led astray, but to be faithful in the face of persecution, materialism and internal dissension.

In the light of the story of the discussion about who were Jesus' family or followers,[10] Mark could also probably see that his readers needed assurance that they were part of God's family even though they were not Jews.

Thus, Mark's purposes were probably not directly evangelistic but pastoral in that he was trying to encourage his readers in their evangelism and life together.

Who are the key personalities in the Gospel?

In the space of just a few pages, Mark introduces many characters, most of them minor ones who come and go in the course of the story: John the Baptist, Simon's mother-in-law, Jairus, Pilate and Herod Antipas are just a few names that appear. Taking a more important role in the story is the crowd which, while not understanding Jesus, at first accepts his ministry. But during Jesus' period of greatest suffering, the crowd is portrayed as identifying with its leaders. These religious leaders are the antagonists in Mark's story. In fact, throughout this Gospel they are depicted in a consistently bad light — as, for example, pretentious, manipulative and blasphemous.

The principal personalities in Mark's story are Jesus and the disciples.

❑ *Jesus*
Jesus, the key person in Mark's story, is portrayed in a number of different ways in this Gospel, each of which helps to create a picture of him for us.

(a) 'Jesus of Nazareth'
This is the typical designation of Jesus as a true human figure.[11] Jesus had a family who believed him to be out of his mind; he got angry and assertive, he became disappointed, and he screamed out in the pain and loneliness of death.[12]

(b) 'Christ'

In Mark Jesus never uses the term 'Christ', God's 'chosen' or 'anointed'[13] of himself. He is reluctant to accept it from others without the qualifications of suffering. Only in the shadow of the cross does Jesus accept the title and Jesus is openly declared 'the Christ, the King of Israel' as he hangs on the cross.[14]

For Mark, the term means that Jesus is God's highest representative or agent for his work of salvation.

(c) 'God's Son'

At key points in the Gospel, Jesus is represented in this way.[15] This description would not have been understood to say anything about his birth, but would show that Jesus had a unique, submissive relationship with God that transcended the confines of human existence and had implications for the welfare of the world.[16]

This name shows that Jesus had been given commanding authority by God to announce and show, in the cure of the demoniacs and healing of the sick, that God's rule over people had become real, though obvious only to those with the eye of trust in God.[17]

The demons are also said to recognise Jesus' true identity, but are not to reveal it, probably because Mark wanted to emphasise that Jesus' identity and mission from God involved suffering and death and too strong an emphasis on his authority from God might undermine their understanding of the need for and purpose of his suffering.[18] Furthermore, the fact that Jesus' identity was known initially only by those other than humans, served to highlight the ignorance of the disciples and the incomprehension of the crowd.

(d) 'Son of man'

This Greek phrase, in Jesus' native language, Aramaic, meant 'as man' and was probably used as an indirect way of referring to oneself. Mark has used the phrase to emphasise the continuity between the humble earthly ministry and suffering of the man Jesus[19] with the one who has the authority of God to forgive sins and will come again in power and judgment.[20]

In the first part of the Gospel, in what appear like case studies on the identity of Jesus, the key issue Mark focuses on is the identity of his main character. In one way or another, four times the question 'Who is Jesus?' is broached. Mark shows his readers that:

* Jesus is the one who has authority over evil spirits (chapter 1, verses 21 to 28)
* Jesus, acting as God, can forgive sins (chapter 2, verses 1 to 12)
* Jesus takes away fear and brings peace and calm (chapter 4, verses 35 to 41)
* Jesus is the one who heals and tells us of God (chapter 6, verses 1 to 6)

✳ Jesus is a teacher (chapter 4, verses 1 to 34). Even though the question of teaching is not raised in this passage, Mark is portraying Jesus as a teacher.

❏ *The disciples*

While Jesus is clearly the central character in Mark's story, the disciples are second in importance. Matthew, Luke and John do not give the disciples such an important role in their stories of Jesus. This raises the question as to why Mark says so much about the disciples and what role they play in his story.

There is the further issue of the kinds of things Mark says about the disciples. For example, the disciples are portrayed as not understanding the teaching of Jesus.[21] They do not understand his attitude to children, his teaching that the rich will find it difficult to enter the kingdom of God, his miracles.

Most importantly, the disciples do not understand what Jesus says about his suffering.[22] A further point of tension is that the disciples fail in their mission to drive out a demon.[23] As dramatic tension rises in the Gospel and the disciples' incomprehension continues, Mark says: 'Judas Iscariot, one of the Twelve, went off to the chief priests in order to betray Jesus to them.' Then, when Jesus is arrested, Mark says: 'They all left him and ran away.'[24]

From all this, a disturbing picture of the disciples begins to emerge. One scholar concluded:

. . .Mark is assiduously involved in a vendetta against the disciples. He is intent on totally discrediting them. He paints them as obtuse, obdurant, recalcitrant men who at first are unperceptive of Jesus' messiahship, then oppose its style and character, and finally totally reject it. As the *coup de grâce*, Mark closes his Gospel without rehabilitating the disciples.[25]

This picture cannot be correct, for there is too much evidence to the contrary. For example, at one point the disciples — whom Mark is identifying with the twelve apostles — return from their preaching and healing mission, apparently quite successful. Also, even though Peter is said to deny Jesus three times, Mark rehabilitates him. Peter breaks down and cries, probably indicating his repentance. Also, there is a message from the empty tomb that the risen Jesus will continue to lead Peter (chapter 16, verse 7).[26]

It has also been suggested that the disciples are cast to represent a group or section of Mark's church which, in turn, he wishes to attack and correct. However, the views of the disciples attacked in Mark — the meaning of the cross, wealth, marriage and divorce, for example — are so wide-ranging and without inner coherence that it is difficult to see that one group could have held all these views. Also, if Mark were attacking a single group, we could expect him to set up and draw attention to some other

group of which he approved.[27]   So the question
remains: What did Mark want his readers to understand or know in the light of his portrayal of the
disciples?

Two points help to answer this question.   First,
there is the telling phrase in chapter 13, verse 37,
which concludes the formal teaching of Jesus in
Mark, where he reports Jesus as saying: 'What I say
to you [the historical disciples], I say to all [that is,
the whole church or, at least, the readers of Mark].'
In other words, what Jesus says to the disciples Mark
intends particularly to be for his readers.

Second, some of the stories of Jesus and sections
of sayings end with instructions intended to train
the disciples.   For example, at the end of the teaching
on divorce, Mark has Jesus give special instruction
to the disciples. Also, the exorcism story in chapter
9 ends with teaching on why the disciples had failed
in healing the boy.[28]

What is the way of discipleship?

When one notices these two features — that Jesus'
teaching of the disciples was for the whole church,
and that even some of the stories of Jesus are told
for training in discipleship — it is not a very big
step to seeing that the important role that Mark
probably had in mind for the disciples was to
portray Christian discipleship.   It is as if Mark is
saying to his readers: 'When you read my book

about Jesus, you will get most out of it if you see yourselves as one of those disciples.' In other words, Mark portrays the disciples as paradigms of aspects of discipleship.

If this analysis is right, then Jesus' followers, today as much as 2 000 years ago, should ask: 'What does Mark say about disciples and discipleship?'[29]

The remaining chapters of this book will answer this question. For the moment, we can anticipate Mark's message and summarise a number of aspects of discipleship to which he draws attention:

* A disciple is someone who is called by Jesus to leave or let go of something or someone in order to follow him.[30]
* A disciple is someone called in order 'to be with Jesus'.[31] The whole of the Gospel portrays a group of people who follow Jesus not at arm's length, but who are constantly with Jesus.
* Discipleship involves not only being with Jesus, but also being sent out on a mission, both to say that people can turn from their sins as well as to cast out demons and heal people.[32]
* The way of discipleship is, as it was for Jesus, the way of the cross. This involves a leaving or saying 'No' to self and taking up one's cross — living deliberately as if in the last hours of life, a life already belonging to another.[33]
* Discipleship is a journey that involves failure, but

also forgiveness. The disciples are portrayed as failing in their mission, in their relationships with each other, and in their confession.[34] But Peter, representing all the disciples, is shown as repentant and the message from the empty tomb is that Jesus will go before or lead the disciples, even Peter.[35]

In the central section of Mark, chapter 8, verse 22 to chapter 10, verse 52, the focus of this book and the most important section of Mark on discipleship, these themes are all highlighted and developed. In this section, Mark has constructed his work so that the motif of discipleship is dependent on Jesus' journey, his nature, his identity and his suffering. But before we explore these things further, we need to take note of the story Mark tells us up to the point of the section on discipleship.

The story so far
Mark does not often describe the inner thoughts and feelings of his characters. Instead, he tells us about the characters through what they say and do. Therefore, if we are to grasp what Mark is saying, we need to pay particular attention to the plot or story line of this Gospel.

❑ *Jesus is introduced (chapter 1, verses 1 to 13)*
The first line of the Gospel reads: 'The beginning of the good news of Jesus Christ, Son of God.'

This 'beginning' is more than a reference to the introduction to the story which follows. The whole of Mark's Gospel is merely a beginning of an unfinished story which goes on after the first Easter to the time of Mark's readers and listeners, stretching right through to the present. What we know and experience of Jesus began with the story Mark is about to tell us.

Mark then says the story we are about to read is 'good news' or 'gospel', *euangelion*. Among Greek people, 'good news' or 'gospel' was a technical word for a messenger's news of victory, particularly in battle. Traditionally, this messenger would be crowned, his spear would be adorned with laurel and he would carry a palm branch. The messenger's very presence brought joy and he was greeted with sacrifices and festivities.

Also important in understanding what Mark had in mind here is that the appearance of an emperor, who was a saviour and god in human form, was said to be good news. The Priene inscription about the emperor Augustus reads: 'The birthday of the god has marked the beginning of the good news for the world.' Also, an emperor's coming of age and accession to the throne were also seen as good news for the world.[36] Mark says that the story of Jesus he is about to relate is 'good news'. He uses this term sparingly and, it seems, strategically — especially in the first chapter.[37] So the good news is, at the same time, the coming of a saviour, Christ, and the coming of God in the form of Jesus the Son of God.

This introduction of Jesus is almost immediately confirmed by no less a person than God when, in the baptism scene, he says that Jesus is his beloved Son in whom he is well pleased.[38] This introduction by God is of fundamental importance to Mark's story for, in all the misunderstanding and rejection of Jesus by various people in the story, the reader knows that this assessment by God is the one that must be held.

With such a brief introduction to Jesus, Mark begins his story in earnest. By way of background, the ministry of John the Baptist is sketched. By drawing parallels between Jesus and John — in their message of repentance and prophecy, having disciples, attracting large numbers of people, suffering under the religious authorities — Mark shows the Baptist to be an able and complete forerunner, preparing people for the coming of Jesus.[39]

❏ *Jesus' work in Galilee (chapter 1, verse 14 to chapter 8, verse 21)*

After the introduction, Jesus breaks through Satan's temptation to remain silent and begins his ministry. The scene of Mark's story turns from the Jordan to Galilee, the scene of the ongoing teaching and activity of Jesus.

The very first activity recorded of Jesus, after the

announcement of his mission in chapter 1, verses 14 and 15, was his choosing some followers. This story is important in Mark's plot, for it sets in train the theme of discipleship. There is both the inherent conflict with and misunderstanding of Jesus on the part of the disciples, and the exasperation on the part of Jesus. The disciples leave behind their livelihood and families to become 'fishers of men'. They are responding to a call from a Jesus about whom they know very little. Then, when Jesus speaks, it is in riddles which they are expected to understand, but do not.

The identity of Jesus is not resolved, but the story's readers and learners know that the point of view they should adopt, set out in the introduction and affirmed by God, is that Jesus is the Son of God. No human being has so far understood this, only the demons. Therefore, Mark implies, the identity of Jesus is only uncovered by supernatural insight.

In this narrative of a very active ministry of continual movement, Mark weaves a multitude of themes — for example, Jesus' battle with the demonic, his conflict with authorities, the nature of the kingdom of God and the misunderstanding of the disciples. This part of the story reaches a climax with the Pharisees asking Jesus for a sign to prove that he is God's chosen agent. At this point, Mark also shows that the disciples still do not understand Jesus and his mission.[40]

Mark then turns to the central section of his story on the nature of true discipleship (chapter 8, verse 22 to chapter 10, verse 52). Here there will be some resolution of the question of Jesus' identity. In the final section of his story (from chapter 10, verse 53 onwards), Mark will tell of Jesus' journey to Jerusalem, his betrayal, arrest, trial, execution and resurrection. In the remaining chapters of this book, we shall be looking carefully at each of the stories in the central section of the Gospel to see, in particular, what Mark wants to tell his readers and listeners about being a follower or disciple of Jesus.

❏ *The way of discipleship (chapter 8, verse 22 to chapter 10, verse 52)*

The section we are studying in Mark begins with a two-stage healing of a blind man at Bethsaida in chapter 8, verses 22 to 26. In view of the idea that receiving sight was a metaphor for the gift of spiritual insight, this story probably represents and draws attention to a gradual enlightenment of the disciples — reflected in the next story and completed by the end of the section (chapter 10, verse 52).

Peter, who was earlier said to have had eyes but not to have seen (verse 18), now confessed Jesus to be the Christ, but did not yet understand or accept the suffering involved in Jesus' mission or purpose. So Jesus went on to give instruction about himself and the nature of discipleship. At the end of chapter 10, there is another healing, this time a complete cure of a blind man who immediately followed Jesus on the road to the cross.

The teaching on discipleship is woven into a story of a journey, with a strong sense of ongoing motion. At the very beginning of the Gospel, Mark cites Malachi 3, verse 1: 'Behold I send my messenger before you, who shall prepare your way.' The implication is that the whole of Jesus' ministry is to be understood as a journey. In this middle section of Mark, the story moves from Bethsaida to Caesarea Philippi, to Capernaum, to Judea, across the Jordan, back to Capernaum and on towards Jerusalem via Jericho.

This movement is encapsulated in the phrase 'on the way' which, apart from chapter 8, verse 3, occurs only in the section of Mark we are studying.[41] In chapter 8, verse 3, Jesus said that, unless he feeds those who come to him, they will faint 'on the way'. It was 'on the way' that Jesus asked his disciples who people said he was and also 'on the way' that the disciples argued about who among them was the greatest.[42]

Mark specifies this 'road' when he says that it was 'on the way to *Jerusalem*' that Jesus again spoke about his death and resurrection. Finally, the phrase occurs in the story of Bartimaeus[43] which comes at the end of the unit on discipleship. So we will see that Mark portrays Bartimaeus as a paradigm of what he wants to say about discipleship.

From the third prediction of Jesus' suffering,[44] and from what immediately follows this middle section — the entry into Jerusalem and the story of the cross — we see that, for Mark and his readers, 'the way' was the way to Jerusalem, the way of the cross: of suffering and eventual glory.

Within this section on discipleship, Mark has used the phrase 'on the way' to tie together and draw attention to the three predictions of suffering and resurrection.[45] The emphasis in these three episodes is on suffering and eventual vindication — and these are seen as an integral part of Jesus' identity, life, mission and destination. In turn, discipleship can only be understood in the light of Jesus' suffering and resurrection, and the way of discipleship itself cannot be understood except as a way of suffering, though followed by eventual glory.

From what has just been said, it may be tempting to suggest that Mark sees discipleship as imitating Jesus. However, we can notice the distance seen between Jesus and his disciples in their respective relationships to God. Jesus is portrayed as having a unique relationship to God.

In the story of Jesus' baptism, this uniqueness is emphasised in saying that the heavens opened, the Spirit descended upon Jesus and a voice came from heaven.[46] The voice itself emphasised Jesus' relationship to God: 'You are my beloved Son. . .' In the transfiguration story, the voice said, 'This is my beloved Son — listen to him.' By way of contrast, there follows the story of the disciples failing to follow Jesus in their healings, so they are to listen to Jesus for instruction.[47]

While the life and ministry of Jesus may be a pattern for the disciples, Mark shows the disciples as failing to be like Jesus. He has a relationship with God in which they are unable to share. While the disciple of a rabbi became a rabbi, or the pupil became a philosopher, the follower of Jesus never became a Christ. The journey is one of imitation, but only partially and in one aspect in particular.[48]

Discussion questions

Talking it through

1 Using the information provided, including the Bible references concerning Jesus' names, what picture of Jesus emerges?

Is there tension in the picture? What picture of Jesus' task comes through?

2 Why are the disciples given such an important role in Mark's Gospel?

3 How does the discipleship of Jesus' followers in Mark differ from each of the following:
(a) the discipleship of Mohammed's followers?
(b) the discipleship of a follower of Karl Marx?
(c) the discipleship of a Jewish rabbi?

4 Why is a journey to Jerusalem such a suitable context in which the events of Mark chapters 8 to 10 take place?

Widening our horizons

1 If it is true that Mark's Gospel was mainly written for Christians, not non-Christians, should it be used today and, if so, how, when speaking to each of the following:
(a) little children?
(b) non-Christians?

2 Mark's Gospel shows the use of 'story' as a teaching tool. There is resistance to moralising today. How is story, therefore, an effective method of teaching? Compare the teaching method used in each of the following:
(a) *Pilgrim's Progress* by John Bunyan
(b) a modern film (some modern American films do this well)
(c) a contemporary children's story you know.
　　Which is the most effective as a teaching tool? What is actually being taught in each (just to test that something *is* being taught!)?

3 How does discipleship differ from other forms of education? Compare it with:

(a) education at a university

(b) apprenticeship for a trade

(c) learning by one- to three-year-olds.

Are those useful comparisons to make? If so, how?

4 'For the disciples Jesus is not the head of a school, but the living Lord' (Gerhard Kittel et al.). If you had been one of the disciples, how would this have affected:

(a) what you would have said about your master?

(b) where you would have said it?

(c) the extent to which you would have gone for it?

Have your conclusions been borne out by history?

1
The blindness
of the disciples

Who is Jesus?
MARK CHAPTER 8, VERSES 22 TO 30

ON THE NOTICEBOARD OF THE Department of Theology at Nottingham University, some wit pinned the following notice:

> 'Who do people say that I am?' Jesus asked.
> 'You are the ground of our being, the apocalyptic realisation and the complete fulfilment of our eschatological expectations,' replied the disciples.
> 'Pardon?' said Jesus.

At the point where we take up his story, Mark has not left the disciples in a very good light. They neither understand Jesus, nor what he can do.

In the preceding story, the disciples had forgotten to bring enough bread.[1] All they had in the boat was one loaf. On two previous occasions, the disciples had been faced with the prospect of feeding large crowds of people.[2] Each time, their resources were meagre — five loaves and two fish for five thousand, and seven loaves and a few fish for seven thousand people. Yet, each time, Jesus took what the disciples had and was able to use it to feed the hungry people.

Now, in chapter 8, verse 15, faced with limited resources, Jesus warned the disciples to beware of the yeast — that is, the empowering resources of the Pharisees. Jesus went on to remind the disciples of what he had been able to do on the two previous occasions similar to this one and said to them, 'Do you have eyes and fail to see?', 'Do you not yet understand?'[3] Despite the disciples' failure here to understand, Jesus' ministry, as well as care and teaching of the disciples, was to continue.

A two-stage healing
(verses 22 to 26)

There are only two stories in the whole of Mark in which Jesus cured blindness. They are both in the middle section of Mark treated in this book.[4] One story, of a two-stage or gradual healing, begins the section of teaching on discipleship to illustrate that

the 'blindness' of the disciples — their lack of understanding — can be changed, even if gradually.

❑ *A difficult journey (verse 22)*
Having most recently returned from the region of Tyre,
they crossed the Sea of Galilee from Dalmanutha
to the other side, arriving in Bethsaida on their way
to Caesarea Philippi, the setting of the next story.[5]

The setting of Bethsaida which Mark has given
this story may have alerted his readers to the significance of the story. A little earlier, Bethsaida was
associated with a difficult crossing of the lake.[6] Also,
along with other early Christians, Mark's readers
may have known that the people of Bethsaida had
been castigated for their lack of belief, even though
they had seen Jesus perform miracles.[7] Thus, in
saying that Jesus and his disciples came to Bethsaida,
Mark may have been alerting his readers to the story
being about difficulties in belief in Jesus.

Blindness was one of the most serious sicknesses
in the ancient world. To be blind was little better
than being dead.[8] Its cure had no precedent in the
Old Testament. So, it was looked forward to in the
messianic age and was a fitting healing to illustrate
the profundity of the spiritual blindness of the followers of Jesus.[9]

❑ *Confidence in Jesus (verse 22)*
The bringing of the blind man to Jesus is not the

first time Mark has shown people so confident in
Jesus' ability that they bring someone to him for
healing. In chapter 2, verses 1 to 12, Mark tells of
four people carrying a paralysed man to Jesus and,
not being able to get near him, they make a hole in
the roof and lower the sick man down to Jesus. On
that occasion, Mark says that when Jesus saw their
trust, he was able to heal the sick man.

Here, in chapter 8, Mark again highlights the role
of the trust of others in Jesus in the healing of a
person. Mark's readers would have noted that the
trust of the blind man's companions involved
'prayer', for it is said they 'begged' Jesus. In the
ancient world, 'beg' (*parakaleō*) included the meaning
of calling on God in times of great need.[10]

Also, Mark has already included touching stories
of, for example, a man with leprosy coming to Jesus
and begging on his knees for healing, and of sick
people begging to touch even the edge of his clothes.
Then, in the story of the healing of the deaf mute,
some people begged Jesus to place his hand on the
sick man.[11] Clearly, from Mark's perspective, the
trust of others and their prayers are important in
Jesus' healing the sick.

❏ *The blind man healed (verses 23-25)*
Why, when generally Jesus performed his healings
in public, should he be said to lead the man out of
the village? Two other stories may help us see what
Mark had in mind.

In the story of the illness and death of Jairus' daughter, Jesus put out the laughing and disbelieving crowd of mourners before healing the girl.[12] It is possible, therefore, that Mark is telling his readers that Jesus wanted to remove the blind man from the unbelieving crowd of Bethsaida.

Another reason might have been the method of healing. In chapter 7, verse 33, the healing of a deaf man with a speech impediment, Jesus removed the man from the crowd and put his fingers in the man's ears, spat, and touched his tongue, saying 'Ephphatha' ('Be opened'). In the story of the blind man we are examining, Jesus is said to put saliva on the man's eyes. Perhaps Mark not only wanted to tell his readers that a lack of trust was an impediment to healing, but that the methods of healing Jesus used should not detract from an understanding that it was Jesus who performed the healing.

In the ancient world, spittle was widely considered to have healing properties. For example, Suetonius, the ancient writer and lawyer, tells of a blind labourer having a dream that he would be healed if Vespasian, the Roman emperor, would consent to spit in his eyes.[13]

The laying-on of hands was also part of healing techniques in the ancient world. For example, in the Dead Sea Scrolls there is a story in which Abraham lays his hands on the king so that he can be healed.[14] The laying-on of hands was thought to transfer healing power — there was a widespread belief that the gods extended their hands to bring health and blessing.[15]

The best illustration of this in Mark is the story of the woman who had suffered from haemorrhages for twelve years. She was healed when she touched Jesus' cloak and Mark says that Jesus was immediately aware that power had gone out from him.[16] That the healing touch was considered effective only in the context of trust in Jesus is clear from this story of the woman with bleeding for, as the disciples say in chapter 5, verse 32: 'You see the crowd pressing in on you; how can you say, "Who touched me?"' Therefore, we can assume that in the story of the blind man, the trust of the blind man, or those who brought him, is important.

Jesus' question 'Can you see anything?' is unique in the healing stories of Jesus. It introduces the most striking aspect of the story. As in the healing of the Gadarene demoniac, the healing takes place in two stages.[17]

The blind man has partially regained his sight as the word 'looked up' (*anablepsas*) shows. Whether or not he had been born blind we cannot tell, for even a blind person would know there are similarities between the human 'trunk' and the 'trunk' of a tree. A second time, Jesus laid his hands on the man. This time the man could see clearly and was able to 'look intently'.

Mark emphasises the thorough success of the cure. He says (in the Greek) that the man was 'restored' and went on 'seeing everything clearly'.

The lack of instant success has been an embarrassment to those who have seen it as a criticism of Jesus' ability to heal.

The two-stage healing has also been a puzzle. Matthew and Luke do not use this story. Perhaps it did not seem honouring to suggest that Jesus' healings were not always instantly successful. Or perhaps it was seen to relate closely to the blindness of the disciples, a theme they did not wish to explore.

The healing cannot have been in two stages because it was thought to be a difficult miracle: stilling a storm or feeding multitudes with next to nothing would have been thought to be much more difficult. Yet, in those, Jesus has been described as instantly successful. One suggestion has been that Mark is portraying Jesus as the great physician. Jesus is shown caring for the man in taking him by the hand and interacting with him until the cure is complete.

It is more likely that the theme of trust and lack of trust is the key to what Mark wants to convey through this two-stage healing.

As this section of teaching on discipleship ends with an instantly successful recovery of sight for a blind man (chapter 10, verses 46 to 52), this story of a two-stage healing may refer to the disciples' gradual understanding of who Jesus is, beginning with their partial understanding of Jesus in the next story.[18] This two-stage or gradual healing is an illustration of what should happen to followers of Jesus.

This story is also an illustration of the miracle required from Jesus before his followers would be able to understand completely who he is and the nature of what it is to follow him. However, we know it did not happen.

In the stories which follow, the disciples of Jesus do not fully understand who Jesus is. The readers of Mark's Gospel know that Judas betrayed Jesus and Peter denied him. They also know that it was only after the death and resurrection of Jesus that his followers truly understood who he was and what he could do. However, by the end of this section, Mark will have given teaching on discipleship and the nature and destiny of Jesus so that the eyes of the disciples could eventually be fully open, even if that was not to happen until after his resurrection.

❏ *The blind man told to go home (verse 26)*
Mark has presented us with another puzzle in this command from Jesus. One long-standing suggestion is that it is a part of Mark's so-called 'secrecy motif'. This suggests that, along with a number of other verses in this Gospel, Mark composed this conclusion to the healing story to explain why Jesus was not more readily and more widely recognised for who he was before the resurrection.[19]

However, this theory has been discredited.[20] Too often, the commands to silence are ignored and Jesus is even depicted as encouraging a healed person to spread the story of what had happened to him rather than keep it quiet as here in verse 26.[21]

It is more likely that Mark is continuing to draw attention to the theme of belief and disbelief associated with Bethsaida in this passage — that is, the man is being asked to disassociate himself from the town, which symbolised disbelief. Also, through this small literary device, Mark is able to pave the way for Jesus to be able to go away alone with his disciples to Caesarea Philippi.

Jesus' asks about himself
(verses 27 to 30)

Apart from the heavenly voice who declared Jesus to be 'my Son',[22] only the demons had shouted out Jesus' true nature up to this point. No human character in Mark's story had so far understood who Jesus is.

However, from now on, while no single character or characters come to understand fully who Jesus is, Mark gives a series of stories — two in this central section of the Gospel — revealing the identity of Jesus.[23] The purpose of this next story, Peter's so-called messianic confession, is to bring to a head the resolution of the conflicting views on Jesus' identity.

The story of Jesus' journey with his disciples

continues. They unexpectedly head forty kilometres north from Bethsaida to the village of Caesarea Philippi. The plural 'villages' probably refers to the villages in the region of Caesarea Philippi. This is a beautiful area at the source of the Jordan on the slopes of Mount Hermon.

There, a little more than a generation previously, Philip the son of Herod the Great and Cleopatra had rebuilt the village of Paneus (modern-day Banias, near the site of a grotto which Herod the Great had consecrated to the Greek god Pan). Philip took up residence in the new city he named in honour of Caesar.[24]

Mark may have intended his readers to see a double significance in this setting for Peter's declaration of Jesus' true identity. On the one hand, it was a place where Herod built a magnificent temple to the emperor Augustus.[25] Also, for the Jews, Caesarea Philippi, populated mainly by pagans, was on the boundary of the Holy Land, on the frontiers of Gentile territory.[26]

In verse 27, Mark uses that ominous phrase 'on the way' when he introduces Jesus' questioning of his disciples. We have seen that Jesus' journey with his disciples to Jerusalem is encapsulated in this phrase. Although the cross is not yet in sight, its dark shadow is being cast over the story.

The shadow of the cross was cast across Mark's story earlier (in chapter 3, verse 6) when the

Pharisees went out and conspired with the Herodians to kill Jesus, after he had healed a man in the synagogue on the Sabbath. So we can see that the revelation of who Jesus is takes place against the background of the journey to the suffering in Jerusalem. We will see this point confirmed in our next chapter.

❏ *How the people saw Jesus*
  (verses 27b and 28)
As a foil or to highlight a contrast, Mark now has the disciples list what are incorrect assessments of Jesus' identity. We know they are incorrect views because Mark has already told us who holds these views and what they mean.

The first response is that Jesus is John the Baptist. In Mark, he is both forerunner and the one who foreshadows the ministry of the Messiah. John is portrayed as fulfilling Isaiah's hope of a new exodus,[27] as well as the expectation of Malachi 4, verses 4 to 5 that the prophet Elijah will return 'to restore all things'.[28] In the very first story about John, 'the leather belt around his waist' identifies him with Elijah.[29] Thus, as forerunner, John prepares God's people for the Messiah by calling them to a baptism related to repentance.[30]

However, John is not only a forerunner. His very life foreshadows the Messiah. He, like Jesus, is sent by God in fulfilment of prophecy, proclaims repentance, is followed by disciples and crowds, prophesies, is rejected by contemporary religious and secular authorities, and is unjustly killed by individuals controlled by others.[31]

Yet, even though Mark portrays Jesus and John in similar ways, right from the start he leaves his readers in no doubt that Jesus is more than John the Baptist: 'The one who is more powerful than I is coming after me; I am not worthy to stoop down and untie the thong of his sandals. I have baptised you with water; but he will baptise you with the Holy Spirit,' says John.[32]

In Mark, Elijah is identified with both Jesus and John the Baptist. From the context here and from the fact of its being an outsider's view,[33] we know that Mark considers it a mistake to identify Jesus with Elijah. However, by having Jesus say that in John the Baptist Elijah has come, Mark signals to the readers that this is the correct view.[34]

The view expressed here (that Jesus was one of the prophets returned at the end of time for a new and final phase of his ministry) is the thought many had — that Elijah, Moses, Enoch or Jeremiah would return.[35] The context of the present passage tells us that this is not the correct view.[36]

From all this, the reader is left to conclude that no human being has been able to discern the correct identity of Jesus, even though the disciples, in particular, are expected to understand.[37]

❏ *How Peter saw Jesus (verse 29)*

The rumours about Jesus' identity which the disciples had just repeated are only partially correct.[38] Now at last, one of the main characters, Peter (representing the disciples), appears to perceive correctly the identity of Jesus.

The term 'messiah' (*mesiha* in Aramaic or *christos* in Greek) meant many different things in the time of Jesus and the early Christians. For example, the Qumran community on the edge of the Dead Sea expected both a royal messiah of the house of David as well as a priestly messiah descended from Aaron. Many Jews at the time expected the Messiah to be a political figure able to reverse Israel's national misfortunes so that it could become a super power in the world.[39] In the light of such views, readers of Mark would not be surprised that no-one in his story had so far realised Jesus' true identity.

However, the word 'messiah' or 'Christ' also carried with it the idea of a figure chosen or 'anointed' (*christos* in Greek) by God with power for special service.[40] Thus, in Mark's story so far, Jesus the Messiah has been portrayed as a teacher and exorcist with an authority unlike his contemporaries, as a healer, and as one who forgives as God forgives. In turn, what Peter has got right — and the readers are therefore to note — is that the political and nationalistic aspects of messiahship are not part of Jesus' role. We will soon see that although Peter's confession is correct, his understanding of it is still inadequate.

There is no doubt for the reader of Mark that 'messiah' is the correct view of Jesus' identity. Ever since the opening lines of the Gospel, the readers have known that Jesus is the Christ or Messiah.[41] Then, in chapter 9, verse 41, Mark will have Jesus affirm this title by indirectly using it of himself.

❏ *How Jesus saw himself (verse 30)*
The command to silence signals to us the validity of Peter's confession. Just as the demons were silenced because they knew him,[42] so Peter had to be silent for he had correctly understood who Jesus is.

The inadequacy of what the readers learnt about Jesus as the Messiah or God's anointed explains why Mark had Jesus order the disciples not to tell anyone about him.[43] While Peter was correct in identifying Jesus as the Messiah, readers of Mark were not to think that what they had so far read about the Messiah was adequate, nor was it to be the basis of their preaching of Jesus.

Discussion questions

Talking it through

1 Do you think a miracle about blindness is an appropriate miracle for Jesus to use to teach his disciples? Why/Why not?

2 Why do you think the disciples found it so difficult to understand Jesus' teaching?

3 Why do you think Peter's response in verse 29 is sometimes called a 'confession', not just a 'reply'? What ideas does that word conjure up for you? Do you think it is an appropriate word?

Widening our horizons

1 Here we have a miracle of two-stage healing and we also have the developing understanding of the disciples — of which the miracle is a picture. How can there be similar links for us:

(a) between dreams and real life?
(b) between conversation and thought?
(c) between reading and thought?
(d) between prayer and life?

Do you think this is coincidental? Does it tell us anything about God's communication with us?

2 Can 'casting pearls before swine' be a legitimate reason for being secretive? In what situations could it be argued by some that secrets should be kept from:

(a) one's children?
(b) one's spouse?
(c) one's employer?
(d) one's employee?

Should secrets *never* be kept from others? If they should be, what questions

should we ask ourselves before deciding to
keep them?

3 Jesus had a clear idea of who he was. Our
security is very much tied up with our identity. How can this explain the following:
  (a) the low esteem of many indigenous
      peoples around the world?
  (b) the low esteem of homeless teenagers?
  (c) the low esteem of many housebound
      women?
  (d) the low esteem of many unemployed
      men?

  In terms of identity and security, how
can such problems be tackled?

4 Silence here and elsewhere plays a significant
role in Jesus' life. Indicate situations that
you know of in your life and that of others
where silence would have been the
appropriate response.

  When, on the other hand, is silence to
be condemned?

2
The demands of Jesus

Who can be a disciple?
MARK CHAPTER 8, VERSE 31 TO
CHAPTER 9, VERSE 1

JOHN CALVIN said:

> Whoever the Lord has adopted and deemed
> worthy of his fellowship ought to prepare them-
> selves for a hard, toilsome and unquiet life.[1]

Three times Jesus was to tell the disciples of his
fate; three times the disciples were to show, by word
and action, that they did not understand Jesus'
predictions; and three times Jesus was to have to
give further instructions to his disciples.

We have just seen, in the last chapter, that Peter's

statement that Jesus is the Christ, the Messiah, was correct, yet inadequate. The inadequacy of the disciples' understanding of Jesus' identity, mission and destiny becomes clear in the story of the first of the three so-called passion predictions — chapter 8, verses 31 to 34.

Who is Jesus and where is he going? (verses 31 to 33)

Mark calls Jesus 'the Son of Man'. This title is the only one directly used by Jesus of himself in this Gospel. It indicates its importance to Mark in what he wants to tell us about Jesus.

❏ *The Son of Man (verses 31 and 32a)*

Whenever characters in this Gospel discuss the question, 'Who is Jesus?', the answer is 'The Son of Man'.[2] Further, when we keep in mind that the other titles Mark uses of Jesus — 'Jesus', 'Christ', 'Son of God' and 'Son of David' — are all qualified in some way, whereas 'Son of Man' is not, we see that this must be the title Mark thinks best describes Jesus.

For example, in the passage we are looking at, Peter calls him 'the Christ'.[3] But it is not adequate, for Mark immediately calls Jesus 'the Son of Man'.[4] And, in the story of the transfiguration, the revelation of Jesus' identity as the 'Son of God' (chapter 9, verse 7) is corrected and overshadowed by his identity as 'the Son of Man'.[5]

What does Mark want us to understand by the term 'the Son of Man'? In popular thinking, even from the second century, the term 'Son of Man' usually denoted the humanity of Jesus over against his divinity.[6] However, even a cursory glance at Mark's Gospel shows that this view does not hold for our writer. In chapter 8, verse 38, for example, the title is used to direct attention to the future heavenly power and glory of Jesus.[7]

We begin to see the meaning of this title in Mark when we notice that, of the fourteen times Mark has Jesus use the title 'the Son of Man', in all but four cases, the shame and suffering of Jesus is closely associated with it.[8] In this title, Mark is telling us that *Jesus' identity cannot be fully grasped apart from taking into account his sufferings and death*. It is in this suffering and death that many will be ransomed.[9] This suffering and death is a part of and prelude to the future coming of Jesus in great power and glory to gather his elect.[10]

Behind the little word 'must' (*dei* in Greek), there is Mark's belief that the suffering and death of Jesus were not some unforeseen monumental mistake. Rather, God's will and purpose were being carried out. In a while, Mark will tell us that even scripture shows that the Son of Man must suffer.[11]

As if to drive home the point that this suffering and rejection is from God, Mark concludes Jesus' statement in verse 32 by saying he spoke 'the word' to them.[12] Mark, along with other early Christians, used this phrase to mean 'preaching the good news of being saved'.[13] Despite first impressions, the rejection, suffering, death and resurrection of Jesus is actually the good news.

❏ *Incomprehension (verses 32b and 33)*
Speaking for all the disciples, Peter expressed incomprehension that the Messiah, God's special messenger, should have to suffer.

By themselves, Jesus' spectacular miracles of healing and exorcism, as well as authoritative command over the forces of nature, were soon to lead to a triumphalist view of Jesus and his mission. We will see this could lead to followers adopting a triumphalist view of discipleship. That is, while the disciples of Jesus were quite able to heal the sick and exorcise the demonised, being a follower of his does not exempt a person from suffering and apparent failure any more than the Son of Man was exempt from rejection and suffering.

Clearly, in this extremely strong rebuke from Jesus, Mark wants to make it absolutely plain that the identity and destiny of Jesus cannot be understood apart from his rejection, suffering and death. To think otherwise is satanic!

Who can be a disciple?
(chapter 8, verse 34)

Since misunderstanding the identity and destiny of
Jesus is to misunderstand what it means to be one
of his followers, who can be a disciple is spelt out
in this verse.

What Jesus has to say about being his follower
is addressed not only to the disciples, who are trying
to understand what their status means, but also to
the crowd of potential followers.[14]

At this point in Mark's story, the crowd of people
mentioned in verse 34 is not characterised as Jesus'
enemy. However, the crowd still stands over against
Jesus in that it neither understands the parables nor
the identity of Jesus.[15] Thus, in having Jesus address
the crowd as well as the disciples, Mark may be
telling us that Peter's incomplete view of Jesus and
discipleship is no further advanced than that of the
uncomprehending crowd whose major response to
Jesus is amazement or astonishment,[16] rather than
trust.

To be a follower of Jesus, Mark says Jesus asks
for two specific or decisive acts as well as a continuous requirement:

If any want to become my followers, let them
deny themselves and take up their cross and
follow me.[17]

This pattern of decisive acts required by Jesus, followed usually by an imperative, is important to Mark's message about being a disciple, for it is found in his other stories of Jesus' calling people to be his disciples.[18]

❏ *First, a disciple forgets self*
  (verse 34)

Jesus' first demand is that disciples deny themselves. The basic idea behind the Greek word *aparneomai* is to say 'No' to self. In other words, a follower of Jesus must disown not just sins and weaknesses, but deny utterly the running of his or her life. The strength of the word 'deny' is seen in the way Mark uses it later in his story. Mark uses the word when Peter is challenged with being with Jesus and is portrayed as denying all knowledge of Jesus.[19] There are three features to note about this demand:

(a) Self-surrender

This self-abandonment is much more radical than any ascetic exercises or trivial 'self-denials' in God's name in the season of Lent.

The legend of the fourth century monk, Telemachus, illustrates the point.[20] He decided to leave the world and to live alone in prayer and fasting in order to find salvation. In his lonely life, he sought nothing but God. However, one day it suddenly dawned on him that his life was based not on a selfless, but on a self-controlled love of God.

So he abandoned his hermit's life and returned to the real world. As it turned out, he became instrumental in putting a stop to the bloodthirsty gladiatorial games in Rome.

This story illustrates that denying oneself is not doing difficult things for God. We can be a good person and have devoted the whole of our lives to working for God and the following of his commands, yet still not have abandoned ourselves to follow Jesus. In chapter 6, we will come to Mark's example of such a person: the so-called rich young ruler. If we have not said 'No!' to the whole of our lives, we have not undertaken a fundamental thing Jesus requires of potential followers. To hang onto the smallest amount of our lives is to control all of our lives.

Dietrich Bonhoeffer, a young theologian martyred by the Nazis in 1945, wrote what is now a famous book, *The Cost of Discipleship*. At one point he says:

> Are you worried because you find it so hard to believe? No-one should be surprised at the difficulty of faith, if there is some part of his life where he is consciously resisting or disobeying the commandment of Jesus.[21]

(b) A command

The tense of the word 'deny' is in the imperative (*aparnēsasthō*). That is, it is a command, a requirement of Jesus that we say 'No' to ourselves if we are to become his follower. The difficulty is that it is not in our natural instincts to abandon our whole selves to anyone, including Jesus. However, if we do not, we lose everything. That is also clear from verse 35.

(c) A decisive act
The word is also in the aorist tense. This indicates that it is a single, initial act of denial made in a point of time. Thus, from Mark's perspective, giving up the running of our lives is not something that we grow into any more than we grow into marriage or opening a bank account. According to Mark, a potential follower of Jesus needs to undertake a decisive act of self-abandonment; it will not just happen.

If this requirement for discipleship, of forgetting self, has to do with our relationship with ourselves, the next requirement has to do with our attitude and relation to Jesus.

❏ Second, a disciple takes up a cross (verse 34)
Popular Christian mythology has reduced the idea of bearing one's cross to descriptions of the unwelcome difficult tasks and burdens of life — putting up with a menial job, acne or an unforgiving mother-in-law! However, taking up our cross is much more difficult and profound than that.

To understand what Mark meant, we need to

keep in mind that it would have been a graphic metaphor not only for Mark's readers, but for all who lived in the Roman world. Josephus, the Jewish historian who was born a few years after the first Easter, gives an insight into the horrors of crucifixion. In his autobiography, he says:

> On my return [to Jerusalem I] saw many prisoners who had been crucified and recognised three of my acquaintances among them. I was cut to the heart and came and told Titus with tears what I had seen. He gave orders immediately that they should be taken down and receive the most careful treatment. Two of them died in the physicians' hands; the third survived.[22]

When crucifixion was a form of execution, the one who took up a cross was a condemned person. Having been condemned to death, the person would have to carry the cross-piece of timber to the place of crucifixion. Thus, in being called to take up his cross, the follower of Jesus was being asked to forfeit his life as Jesus did. Life was to be given over into the hands of another. That is, one lived, yet one's life belonged to another.

In short, for Mark and his first readers, to take up one's cross was to live deliberately as in the last hours of life — a life already belonging to another.

There is, however, a fundamental and remarkable difference between the image of crucifixion conveyed from this infamous form of death sentence and what Jesus says here about what potential disciples are to do. Whereas the taking up of a cross was expected and demanded of the condemned criminal, followers of Jesus were expected to take up their cross *voluntarily*!

The metaphor of carrying one's cross makes it clear that, for Mark, following Jesus was (and is) not adhering to a particular set of teachings which is to be carefully preserved, interpreted and handed on to later devotees. Discipleship is not even primarily conforming one's behaviour to a set of ethical maxims.

If we may glance across to Paul, we see that he has summed up the idea well when he says: 'It is no longer I who live, but it is Christ who lives in me. And the life I now live in the flesh I live by faith in the Son of God, who loved me and gave himself for me.'[23]

The grammar of Mark's text does not rule out the idea that he was thinking of the need for repeated decisive acts of taking up one's cross (and even denying oneself). Luke spells this out by saying that if any wanted to follow Jesus, they would need to 'take up their cross daily'.[24]

❏ *Third, a disciple follows Jesus (verse 34)*
So far, Mark records Jesus asking potential disciples to undertake two decisive acts. Then, in the last part of Mark 8, verse 34, Jesus issued a continuous

requirement: 'Follow me!' (*akoloutheitō*). The previous requirements have been in the aorist tense;
this one is the present tense: 'Go on following me.'
It may be that Mark is saying that becoming a
disciple of Jesus involves an initial set of two
decisive actions followed by an ongoing process
of following.

This command to follow Jesus could be taken in
one of two ways. It could be that, having said 'no'
to the running of our lives and having taken up our
cross, we are only then in a position to follow Jesus.
Alternatively, even if initially the denying of self and
taking up of one's cross preceded the following, they
are all continuous or repeated events required of a
disciple. In any case, we know at least that the
following is a continuous requirement. We also
know that this following is compulsory, for the Greek
tense is an imperative. That means that the following is demanded and is a continuous act rather than
a series of individual decisive acts.

Jesus is not asking his disciples to consult him at
various times, but to stay with and follow him at
all times. When Jesus was with his disciples, he did
not only tell them things, but lived, ate, healed and
preached with them. And the disciples did not visit
Jesus occasionally and ask his advice; they followed
him.

In short, if we have given up the control of our
lives, if we have given our lives over into the
hands of Jesus, we can and are to follow him, to

be preoccupied by him — and he is to be pre-eminent for us.

The alternative to being a disciple (verses 35 to 38)

The seriousness of these demands is now underlined in three separate sayings. Each of these sayings begins with 'for' (*gar* in Greek) showing that they are explaining the central saying of Jesus. Each of these sayings puts the other side of the coin — the 'or else' of the hard saying in verse 34.

❏ *Lose your life! (verses 35 to 37)*
The first part of this explanatory saying about living as if in the last hours of life puts Jesus' call to follow him in relief. An attempt in the present to hang on to one's life (to save it) will, in the future, end up meaning losing life. The second part of this saying explains Jesus' call positively: saving one's life comes about through losing it now for the sake of Jesus and the gospel.

The statements about losing one's life for the sake of Jesus, as well as for the sake of the gospel, are most probably intended to be one and the same. The same phrase — 'for the sake of the good news' — occurs in chapter 10, verse 29. Then, on two occasions, preaching the gospel is explicitly referred to as the activity of the church after Easter, which involved suffering and persecution.[25]

To 'lose one's life' — metaphorically or literally — by following Jesus is, in fact, to save one's life.[26] To follow Jesus involves both the task of preaching the good news of the coming of Jesus and the demand to turn from sin.

The second explanatory saying shedding light on the meaning of Jesus' call to the crowd and his disciples to follow him comes in two parts. Again, following Jesus is put in terms of a life-or-death option. In short, to be able to amass the wealth of the entire world and not become a follower of Jesus would still mean forfeiting one's life. It is not possible to talk in terms of an earthly price large enough to secure one's life.

This metaphor from the commercial world was obviously appropriate for Mark's readers for, a little later, he shows a wealthy man losing his life by choosing wealth.[27]

❏ *Jesus will be ashamed of you!*
  (verse 38)
A final saying is used to drive home the gravity of Jesus' demand on potential followers.

Some scholars have used this verse to argue that Jesus is to be distinguished from 'the Son of Man' who was an end-time figure. This was almost certainly not Jesus' view.[28] If Jesus had spoken of figures other than himself, the Christians after Easter would not have identified the risen Lord with Jesus, but waited for another agent from God. And we have no evidence from this Gospel that Mark thought the Son of Man was anyone other than Jesus. We, the readers, now know that 'Son of Man' means 'messiah'. We can, then, take the saying as it stands as a reference to Jesus the Messiah coming in judgment in the glory of God.

What Mark probably means by this verse is that, if a potential follower of Jesus cannot follow him in *suffering* as Jesus now suffers, then that person will not share the *glory* that is to be Jesus' in the future.

A note of encouragement (chapter 9, verse 1)

So far Mark has spelt out clearly the high cost of following Jesus and the even higher cost of *not* following Jesus. The final saying in this section is the positive aspect of Jesus' demand, a way of encouraging his disciples and potential followers.

Precisely what Mark had in mind in this verse is a puzzle. Mark could have expected the end of the world to take place in the lifetime of the disciples. However, for Mark, the coming of the kingdom of God with power is not the second coming. We know from his introduction that the coming of Jesus was the coming of the kingdom of God.[29] And, we have just seen in verse 38, that the second coming is described in terms of angels and glory. Most likely, Mark understands the coming of the kingdom of God *with power* to refer to the transfiguration story which follows.[30]

*   *   *

The kind of discipleship Mark is portraying would have been as profoundly challenging to Mark's first readers as it is to us. We, in the twentieth century, need to note that, for Mark, discipleship was not essentially reforming society or alleviating its suffering. Discipleship was and is about a deep personal loyalty to Jesus, which means living for him, not for ourselves.

While the Jewish rabbis had their pupils and the Greek wandering philosophers their disciples, no follower was expected to offer — and receive — so much as a follower of Jesus. As in the case of God's call to the Old Testament prophets, Jesus demands an absolute break with all other loyalties, yet he brings the disciple into an intimate relationship with him and other disciples to be involved in God's work in the world.[31]

We now turn to Mark's story of the transfiguration to face the question: Is there glory without suffering for Jesus?

Discussion questions

Talking it through

1 Why is the term 'Son of Man' for Jesus so crucial in Mark's Gospel? What is particularly appropriate about such a way of expressing Mark's idea?

2 What does Jesus mean, in verse 33, by saying Peter is putting his mind on human, rather than divine things? What does this comment suggest about what 'divine things' are like? Can we understand them?

What, precisely, don't we understand about what Jesus says in verse 31?

3 What is particularly difficult about the decision to take up our cross being *voluntary*? Why would anyone bother doing it? Why have followers of Jesus bothered doing it in the past?

4 How important would such events as Jesus'
   miracles and the transfiguration have been to
   the disciples? How would they have helped
   to keep them going? Have we equivalent
   means of encouragement?

Widening our horizons

1 A designation like 'Son of Man' indicates a great deal about Jesus' worldview.

What worldview lies behind each of the following designations:
(a) 'a knight of the realm'?
(b) 'the honourable member'?
(c) 'working class'?
(d) 'priest'?

What worldview lies behind Jesus' term 'Son of Man'?

2 What is the difference between a selfless and a self-controlled love of God? Think of specific directions we can take in each of the following areas to ensure that we don't fall into the pitfall of self-controlled love:
(a) prayer and devotional life
(b) service for others
(c) church commitments
(d) career commitments

3 Think of examples, real or imaginary, where denial for Christ has brought its own rewards:

(a) in Third World service
(b) in support for the needy and weak in
     your neighbourhood/family
(c) in self-effacing work.

Is the actual action an adequate sign of
denial? Or is it necessary to look at motiva-
tion as well?

4 Why is life so hard? In your answer, show
what God is like, what the world is like and
what our place in the scheme of things is.

If you had your complete choice, how
would you change things?

3

The transfiguration
of Jesus

What did Jesus want his disciples to know?
MARK CHAPTER 9, VERSES 2 TO 13
'Joy & Woe are woven fine'
William Blake

THE MENTION OF WHAT IS KNOWN as 'the
transfiguration' taking place 'six days later'[1] marks
a new and important stage in Mark's story. Mark
has set the scene in having Jesus affirm the disciples'
recognition that he is the Messiah.

Jesus has also been depicted as transforming the
disciples' understanding of messiahship to the point
where they could become discouraged. Hence, there
was the note of encouragement found in chapter 9,

verse 1 about some of the disciples being able to see that the kingdom of God had come with power.

Now, for their further encouragement and development, Peter, James and John are going to see that the reign of God in Jesus has come with power. They are about to have their earlier confession confirmed that Jesus is God's anointed one. They are about to be the first human beings to hear what, so far, only Jesus has heard and only the demons know.[2]

Jesus is transfigured on the high mountain (verses 2 to 8)

Only in chapter 14, verse 1 is Mark as precise with his timing as he is here with the mention of 'six days later' (verse 2) for the transfiguration. Mark's readers would quite likely have seen in this phrase an echo of the Old Testament story of cloud covering Mount Sinai for six days, after which God spoke to Moses out of the cloud on the mountain.[3]

❏ *The setting (verse 2a)*
The high mountain setting of this story would have confirmed for Mark's readers that Moses' story was significant in understanding the story they were about to read. As the story of Moses shows, a mountain was the place where God spoke to his special messengers.[4]

The three chosen to accompany Jesus here, Peter, James and John, were chosen to accompany him on three previous occasions. In chapter 5, verse 37, when Jesus wanted to exclude those lacking trust in him, these were the only disciples to accompany him with the parents to the place where he was to raise the little girl to life.

In chapter 13, verse 3, Jesus was again on a mountain and about to speak of the destruction of Jerusalem and the future in answer to a private question from Peter, James and John. In chapter 14, verse 33, Peter, James and John were the only disciples chosen to be near Jesus when he was praying in the garden before he was arrested.

Perhaps we are to conclude that, when these three were with Jesus, Mark thought he was involved in something of the highest significance requiring the company of those who trusted him most. In line with this, Mark says Jesus led them 'apart, by themselves,' a double expression characteristic of Mark.[5]

❏ *The transfiguration (verses 2b and 3)*
The word 'transfiguration' arises from the Latin *transfiguratus*, the Vulgate Bible's translation of the Greek *metamorphoō*, meaning 'to assume a different form'. The clothes are literally said to be 'dazzling white, such as no fuller on earth could bleach them'.[6] That is, they are described as glittering like a polished brass or gold surface.[7]

A fuller (*gnapheus*) was a bleacher who cleaned woollen cloth with nitrium.[8] In the clothes being so described, the supernatural origin of the transfiguration is being affirmed.

In Jewish apocalyptic literature of the period, descriptions of such changes of people and their clothing are used to describe the glory of the Messiah.[9] Thus, what the transfiguration would have meant for Mark and his readers would be that here was a revelation of the messianic yet hidden glory of Jesus. In other words, the disciples were able to catch a glimpse or foretaste of Jesus in all his glory at the *parousia*, the coming again of Jesus.

❑ *A wrong response to a vision (verses 4 to 6)*
From the way 'appeared' (verse 4) is generally used in the New Testament, Mark probably means that Elijah and Moses appeared to the disciples in a vision, talking to Jesus.[10]

Peter's response to seeing Jesus transformed and talking with Elijah and Moses was to say that it was good that the disciples were there, for they could make three dwellings or tents (*skēnas*) for them.[11] These tents were most probably intended to be temporary dwellings of thatched or plaited branches erected for the joyous Feast of Booths or Tabernacles.[12]

However, Mark obviously considers Peter's response to be wrong. The same words 'did not know what to say' are used here in verse 6 and in chapter 14, verse 40. There, Peter, James and John had fallen asleep in the garden of Gethsemane when they were told to stay awake. This is another occasion when these three followers let Jesus down.

The nature of Peter's error is seen in Mark saying, 'They were terrified' (*ekphobos*). Although this is the only time this particular word for 'fear' is used in Mark, a similar noun (*phobos*) is used of the disciples' fearful and questioning response to Jesus calming the storm.[13]

The fact that fear or terror is inappropriate (and the opposite to trust and understanding) is made clear in Jesus' words to the synagogue ruler: 'Do not fear, only believe.'[14] Similarly, on seeing Jesus walking on the water, the disciples are reported to be terrified[15] and, as we will see in the next chapter of our study, on hearing that Jesus would be killed and rise after three days, 'they did not understand what he was saying and were afraid to ask him'.[16]

What is Peter's error? What is it he had not understood? It could be that he had misunderstood the identity of Jesus and treated him as an equal of Elijah and Moses. This is unlikely, for Peter had already declared that Jesus is the Messiah rather than someone like Elijah and Moses.[17] And even Peter's use of the apparently common title 'Rabbi' or 'Teacher' for Jesus is, for Mark, a title of unusual respect, as we will see when it is used by Mark's model disciple in chapter 10, verse 51.

More likely, in view of Mark's larger interest, the

error represented in Peter's response is, again, the desire to capture and maintain a glimpse of the coming of the kingdom with power, isolated from shame, suffering and death. Peter has not learnt that there is no glory without suffering for Jesus. He represents those who want the glory of victory without the battle being fought and won.

❑ *In the powerful presence of God and his Son (verse 7)*

The cloud overshadowing Jesus and the disciples is another echo of the Old Testament story of God calling to Moses out of the cloud on Mount Sinai.[18] More significantly, the only other times Mark mentions clouds have to do with the future power and glory of the Son of Man.[19] In other words, Mark is again drawing attention to the fact that this is a story showing that, in Jesus, the reign of God has come with power.[20]

The climax of the story of the transfiguration is reached in verse 7: '. . . from the cloud there came a voice, "This is my Son, the Beloved; listen to him!"'

God only speaks twice in Mark's story — in very similar terms — and each time he affirms Jesus to be his Son: at the baptism and here in the transfiguration.[21] However, instead of the words being for Jesus as they were at his baptism, here they are spoken directly to the disciples.

So far, Jesus' sonship has not been clear to human

observers. Apart from God, the only other characters, so far, to call Jesus God's Son are the demons.[22]
As we have suggested, this probably tells the reader
that Jesus' true identity is something hidden, requiring supernatural knowledge to comprehend.

At last, one of the human characters in Mark's
story has a direct revelation and confirmation of the
identity of Jesus. God is clarifying and supplementing
Peter's recent confession that Jesus is the Messiah.

Of all the titles used of Jesus, 'Son of God' stands
out as having special significance for Mark. It may
have been part of Mark's first line, 'The beginning
of the Gospel of Jesus Christ, Son of God.'[23] As was
noted in the *Introduction*, 'Son of God' is pre-eminent-
ly the title and understanding of Jesus the readers
of Mark know they should adopt because it is the
view God adopts in this story.

When the plot turns to the suffering of Jesus,
the high priest asks Jesus if he is the Son of the
Blessed One.[24] It is as if Mark is signalling to the
readers that now that Jesus is involved in suffering,
the complete picture of his sonship is recognisable.
This view is confirmed by the centurion attending
the crucifixion when he remarks upon seeing the
way Jesus died: 'Truly this man was God's Son.'[25]

The purpose of the title is to draw attention to
the intimate relationship Jesus has with God, his
Father. Thus, each time God designates Jesus as his
Son, the term 'beloved' or 'dear' (*agapētos*) is used.[26]

Mark also tells the touching story of an only, loved son killed while he was collecting rent for his father. The story is told to reflect the intimate relationship between God and his Son.[27] It also draws attention to the authority God has invested in Jesus. In the story, the son — acting for the father — is the heir and is expected to inherit the father's property.

Thus, Mark depicts the demons as recognising that Jesus had come as an envoy from God in bringing about their destruction and taking power over the lives they had, so far, controlled.[28]

To summarise, what is being revealed about Jesus in his ministry causes his followers to confess that he is the Messiah, God's chosen messenger. Also in this story, Mark is telling his readers that what is being revealed about Jesus shows that, from God's perspective, they are dealing with his beloved Son.

There is probably an independent story of the transfiguration in 2 Peter 1, verses 16 to 18. In comparing the words from God in the two stories, the phrase 'listen to him' is unique to Mark and therefore, most likely, significant for him.

For Mark, the words 'hear' or 'listen' contain the Old Testament meaning of 'understanding and obedience'.[29] So he says that Jesus spoke the word in parables to the people in a way that they could 'hear', that is, understand it.[30] And twice he has the phrase, 'let anyone with ears to hear listen', where 'hearing' includes the meaning of 'obedience' as well as 'understanding'.[31] Notably, this emphasis on 'hearing' and 'understanding', with the strong connotation of obedience, are associated with the disciples' failure in these areas.[32]

It is an important theme of discipleship in this section of Mark that understanding who Jesus is carries with it the need to hear and obey him.

For Mark, the prophecy of Deuteronomy 18, verses 15 to 20 has been fulfilled. A prophet has been raised up in whose mouth God has put his words and whose words must be obeyed. Perhaps Mark's readers have been preoccupied with John the Baptist and the Old Testament law and prophets. However, says Mark, God wants to be heard and obeyed through attention to Jesus, who supersedes all these. 'When he commands them to hear him,' says John Calvin, 'he sets him in authority as the highest and unique Teacher of his church.'[33]

❏ *Jesus remains with his followers (verse 8)*
The story ends with Mark saying that suddenly, on looking around, they could no longer see anyone. Jesus only was 'with them'.

Peter, James and John have had an extraordinary experience — probably a vision in which they have caught a glimpse of Jesus in his power and glory and heard God declare him to be his beloved Son. Yet, just as they have been called to be with Jesus, he — despite his glory — remains with his followers.

Jesus reflects on his suffering and glory (verses 9 to 13)

Of the many commands to silence in Mark, the one in verse 9 is unique in setting a time limit to their silence.

Why can't the three disciples declare all that they have seen and heard? After all, they have heard God affirm Jesus' filial relationship with him and that he is to be obeyed. Quite simply, because they would be conveying a notion of Jesus' sonship divorced from the shame and suffering of the cross.

Earlier injunctions to silence were Mark's way of showing that the miracles were not to be used as mere propaganda. Similarly, this command to silence is a warning to his readers not to divorce the suffering from their understanding of the power and glory of the coming Lord Jesus.

The disciples are said to keep 'the matter' or 'word' (*ho logos*) to themselves.[34] Using the phrase 'the word' would have conveyed a double meaning to Mark's readers. On the surface, the disciples are portrayed as keeping silent about the matter they have just witnessed. At another level, the disciples keep silent about 'the word' or 'gospel'[35] which they could not fully understand until after the resurrection.

The appearance of the title 'Son of Man' in verse 9 reinforces for the readers the intrinsic link between the suffering and glory of Jesus and, in a piece of

reverse psychology, challenges readers to proclaim
the shame, suffering and death of Jesus as much as
his triumphant power and coming glory first evident
in the resurrection, though already glimpsed in the
transfiguration.

The puzzle of the disciples is not over the idea
of a resurrection. It was not a new idea.[36] Rather,
the ongoing puzzles were that the Messiah should
suffer and the significance of the resurrection. Would
the resurrection be the so-called 'second coming' or, as
the readers of Mark knew, be separate from it?

The question of the disciples about the coming
of Elijah in verse 11 is probably to be understood as
follows. Mark's readers knew from Malachi 4, verse
5 that Elijah's remaining task was to come and
prepare people for salvation by calling people to
repentance.[37] Indeed, if Elijah is to return — as the
scribes assert — and if people repent, how is it
comprehensible for scripture to say that the Messiah
is to go through many sufferings and be treated with
contempt? Here Mark would have in mind Isaiah
53, verse 3: 'He was despised and rejected by others;
a man of suffering and acquainted with infirmity.'

Speaking perhaps for his readers, Mark is saying
that the three disciples' vision of Elijah as well as of
Moses in the transfiguration heralds the triumphant
coming of the Messiah. Jesus' response in verse 12
is that Elijah has indeed come ahead of the Messiah
to restore all things. This was even hinted at in

chapter 1, verses 2 to 8.

However, he is not the Elijah of the transfiguration; he is John the Baptist, whose preparation for the Messiah was to suffer in the same way as the Messiah was to suffer. Scripture even writes of such suffering by Elijah. Like John the Baptist, he suffered at the hands of an immoral woman and a weak king.[38]

Discussion questions

Talking it through

1 Why do you think Peter, James and John are the ones chosen to go with Jesus up the high mountain?

2 Why do you think the transfiguration took place at this point of Jesus' ministry? What does it tell us about Jesus?

3 What techniques does Jesus use in tackling the difficult task of changing entrenched ways of thinking — in this case, over the idea of a suffering Messiah? Look particularly at verses 7, 9, 12 and 13.

4 Why does Jesus refer to himself twice as the Son of Man (in verses 10 and 12), even though God had referred to him before this in verse 7 as *his* Son?

Widening our horizons

1 The transfiguration is yet another of the
endless range of options God uses in encouraging us. Explore at least one
example from your own or others' experience
of how each of the following has been a help:
   (a) other people's behaviour
   (b) readings from the Bible
   (c) dreams and visions
   (d) personal prayer and meditation
   (e) inspiration from nature
   (f) other people's advice
   (g) other sources.
      How, precisely, has each helped?

2 Here are some statements which, while true,
can easily slip into Peter's error in verse 5.
What else needs to be said to make sure
they are not misunderstood:
   (a) 'Christ gives us victory.'
   (b) 'God gives blessing to all who ask him.'
   (c) 'Christ can take away your pain — if
      you but ask him.'

3 The statement 'I hear you' is now a common way of acknowledging that we are listening. Does this necessarily mean obedience? Should it? What is the type of 'hearing' that you believe should apply in the following cases?

(a) An instruction from God

(b) Advice from a friend

(c) Direction from a political party on how to vote

(d) The sales pitch by an insurance company.
What is the basis on which we should decide how far to take our 'hearing'?

4 The whole of this section of Mark is an exercise in changing entrenched patterns of thinking. What is the most effective way of doing this? Compare Jesus' way of tackling the problem in Mark with that used by, say:

(a) TV evangelists

(b) counselling

(c) TV debates

(d) any other method you can think of.

4
The failure of
the disciples

Why did the disciples fail in their mission?
MARK CHAPTER 9, VERSES 14 TO 29

AFTER PETER'S DECLARATION THAT JESUS was the
Messiah, Mark spelt out the implication of this for
Jesus as well as for his followers. Then, after the
declaration by God that Jesus was his Son and therefore heir, Mark spelt out the implication for Jesus:
suffering and then glory. Now, Mark spells out the
implications for the disciples of Jesus' being God's
Son and heir.

We will learn that following Jesus involves receiving authority and trust, as well as using prayer as
a method of exorcism. Failure of discipleship will
not be a failure to understand the identity of Jesus

or a failure to understand the cost of discipleship.
The failure will be in being unable to carry out the
ministry to which followers of Jesus have been called.

Equipped for mission

In chapter 3, verses 13 to 19a, Mark depicts Jesus
calling to him those he wanted as his followers. We
gather that this is a very significant story, for Mark
says the disciples were chosen on a mountain. We
have seen that in the Old Testament this was an
image signifying an event of divine significance.

The story of Jesus' call of the disciples has some
important implications for this story in chapter 9:

* Those chosen number twelve. With the number
  of tribes of Israel being twelve, the twelve disciples are probably representative of the church.
* The Twelve are given a missionary role in that
  they are called 'apostles' (*apostoloi*), that is,
  'ambassadors' or 'delegates' sent on a mission
  with the power and authority of the one sending
  them — in this case, Jesus.
* The apostles are chosen to be with Jesus. So,
  thereafter, the picture we get in Mark is of a group
  of people 'with him', so that Jesus is almost always depicted being followed by the disciples.
* The followers of Jesus are called not only to be
  with Jesus, but to be sent out with a message.
* They have authority to cast out demons.

From this point until the Twelve are actually sent out on a mission in chapter 6, verse 7, they are shown to be with Jesus, hearing and observing his ministry. They hear the debate about the Holy Spirit being the source of Jesus.[1]

They hear Jesus affirm that those who are obedient to God can belong to him as members of his family.[2]

They hear the teaching in parables about the mysterious way that some respond and others do not respond to the good news.[3]

In this learning period, the disciples also observe a number of miracles of Jesus which demonstrate his ability to bring peace in a storm (perhaps an illustration of how Jesus cares for the church), his ability to cast out demons, to raise the dead and to heal the sick.[4] No wonder Mark concludes this cycle of stories by having people say, 'Where did this man get all this? What is this wisdom that has been given to him? What deeds of power are being done by his hands?'[5]

Having seen and heard the ministry of Jesus, the disciples are sent out with authority to undertake the same kind of ministry.[6] We gather from a hint in chapter 6, verse 30 that they were successful in their task, for Mark says: 'The apostles gathered around Jesus, and told him all that they had done and taught.' However, the first time Mark gives us a specific story of their ministry (here in chapter 9, verses 14 to 29), it is one of utter failure.

An argument about authority (verses 14 to 16)

When Jesus, with Peter, James and John, rejoined the
other nine disciples, they saw a large crowd around
them and some scribes arguing with them. When
(in chapter 9, verse 16) Jesus asked about the nature
of their argument, the answer did not, at first, seem
entirely appropriate, for someone in the crowd
answered for the disciples, saying that his disciples
were unable to cast out a demon.

❏ *Jesus' authority*

However, on closer examination, this answer is entirely appropriate. The first time Mark records that
Jesus taught and performed an exorcism, a discussion was sparked off about his authority being
different from the scribes'.[7] There, the source of
Jesus' authority is the Holy Spirit and Mark emphasises by repetition that this unscribe-like
authority has been given to the disciples for their
ministry.[8] It would not be surprising, then, that in a
story of the disciple's failure in the use of this unique
authority, Mark means us to understand that the
discussion with the scribes was about this authority.

❏ *The disciples' authority*

That the issue in the early part of Mark's story here
is about the nature and source of the disciples'
authority may be confirmed by what he goes on to
say. When the crowd saw Jesus, they were imme-

diately overcome with 'awe' and ran to greet him.[9]
If we look carefully at Mark's use of 'awe', we see
it contains a strong element of distress and is probably
better translated 'perplexed'.[10]

Could it not be that Mark is saying the crowd
was perplexed at the disciples' failure — in the light
of the debate they heard with the scribes about
authority the disciples had received from someone
who so obviously had authority to heal?

Even though it is possible Mark had in mind the
response to Moses on his return from conversing with
God on Mount Sinai,[11] this contrast between the
authority of Jesus and the powerlessness of the disciples in their mission fits the themes of the story better.

A boy possessed (verses 17 and 18)

The father described his son's illness in verse 16.
He was a demon-possessed person whose symptoms
are not always obvious. The same was true of the
demoniac who confronted Jesus in the story of Jesus
in the Capernaum synagogue. If the symptoms had
always been obvious, it is unlikely he would have
been permitted entry to the synagogue.[12]

The symptoms that are described in this story —
being seized, thrown to the ground, foaming and
grinding his teeth and becoming rigid — are similar
to those found in contemporary descriptions of
demon possession.[13] The father finished his description by saying, 'I asked your disciples to cast it out,
but they could not do so.'[14]

The word Mark uses for the disciples' inability is *ischuō* ('to be strong' or 'to have ability'). It has a similar meaning to the word 'to be able' (*dunamai*) in verses 22 and 23. However, a careful look at the way Mark uses *ischuō* shows that it carries with it the idea of self-generated or innate strength.[15]

In other words, the father said that the disciples did not possess the inner strength to perform the exorcism. However, from what Mark has said about the disciples' source of ability as exorcists, they are not expected to have the self-generated strength for such a ministry. Is it any wonder, then, that Jesus is reported as being angry?

The disciples must trust (verse 19)

It is not exactly clear who Jesus then addressed when he said, 'You faithless generation, how much longer must I be among you? How much longer must I put up with you?' However, in that he addresses 'them', and the disciples are one of the important centres of attention in the story, Jesus was most likely intended to speak to them. The subject of Jesus' exasperation also most naturally applies to the disciples' failure.

Jesus had called the disciples to be with him. But they were also called to be sent out on mission. In exasperation Jesus twice asked, rhetorically, how much longer did he need to be with them or bear with them for them to learn. For they remained without trust (*apistos*). They had been given power and authority for such a ministry that depended on being empowered by the Holy Spirit, not on their self-generated or innate strength.[16]

Clearly, Mark considered that faith on the part of the disciples in the commissioning by Jesus would have enabled them to perform the exorcism.

A dramatic confrontation (verses 20 and 21)

Jesus took control of the situation and asked the boy to be brought to him, perhaps by the disciples. Interestingly, it is specifically said that, immediately the spirit saw Jesus, it convulsed the boy.

Again, this same feature is found in the story of the demoniac in the synagogue, in the report of healings by Lake Galilee and in the account of the Gadarene demoniac.[17] It is also found in stories of other ancient exorcists as well as today. Many of those involved in Christian exorcism today confirm that one of the indications of a person being demon-possessed is an adverse, even violent reaction to the presence of Jesus, either in corporate worship or the use of Jesus' name.

In every story Mark has of demon-possession and exorcism, the consternation on the part of the demons or demoniac was a recognition of the power-authority of Jesus as an exorcist to defeat and expel the evil spirit.

The father trusts Jesus' ability
(verses 21 to 24)

In verse 21, Jesus inquired about the origin of the sickness. In the father's reply we not only learn more about the destructive nature of the demon, but also of his cry for help.

The father said, '. . .if you are able. . . help us' (chapter 9, verse 22). It is interesting that Mark does not use the same word 'to be strong' (*ischuō*) that was used of the disciples.[18] Instead, the word here is *dunamai* which, though similar to *ischuō*, can be translated as to be 'able' or 'powerful' with sense of choice or possibility included. That is, in contrast to the failure of the disciples' self-generated strength, the father asked Jesus to choose to do what he recognised he had the ability or power to do.

Then, Jesus said that whether or not he was to heal the boy did not depend on his ability — which all Mark's readers know is not in question — but on trust or faith in that ability. From the story so far, Mark's readers would see this not only as addressed to the father. It was also a reflection on the cause of the disciples' failure. They did not believe or trust that Jesus had given them the authority and ability to perform the exorcism.

The father's immediate response was to cry out, 'I believe; help my unbelief!' (verse 24). This confession of faith exonerated him from the cause of the failed healing and reinforced the disciples' culpability. It was also a reminder to Mark's readers that although people are, of themselves, capable of responding to Jesus in trust, that trust needs supplementing.[19] Again a comment from Calvin is helpful:

> He declares that he *believes*, and yet acknowledges himself to have *unbelief*. These two statements appear to contradict each other, but there is none of us that does not experience both of them in himself. As our *faith* is never perfect, it follows that we are partly *unbelievers*; but God forgives us, and exercises such forbearance towards us, as to reckon us believers on account of a small portion of faith.[20]

Jesus the exorcist (verses 25 to 27)

Mark says that Jesus acted in healing when he saw that the crowd came 'running together'.[21] This is a puzzling comment, for this word *episuntrechō* is not known in any other ancient Greek literature. It could be that Mark was saying that the crowd was about to attack the boy or even Jesus. But there is no evidence for this.

More likely, Mark meant that the members of the crowd, which in Mark's story were observers of all that had happened, are to be understood as coming closer to observe Jesus' techniques — an indication that they misunderstood the nature of his healing.[22]

Jesus' words to the demon were very much the

same as words of other exorcists of the time. Lucian of Samosata, Apollonius of Tyana and Jewish rabbis used similar words to cast out demons.[23]

However, the decisive difference between Jesus' method and others is in his use of 'I'. So far as I can discover, there is no evidence in all the ancient literature we have of an exorcist deliberately and specifically drawing attention to himself in his own ability to cast out demons as Jesus did here. What this means is that, while Mark believed that in his exorcisms Jesus was empowered by the Holy Spirit, he was also telling his readers that Jesus was an extraordinarily powerful exorcist.[24]

Mark's description of the departure of the demon would have been familiar to his readers from what happened when other healers performed exorcisms.[25]

In verse 27, the taking of the boy's hand would have been understood not simply as an encouraging touch, but a means of transferring strength to the sick person. We have come across this notion in Mark 8, verse 22 and it is also found elsewhere in Mark.[26]

Not only did Jesus take the boy's hand; he also 'lifted him up' — the same word Mark used for Jesus being raised from the dead in chapter 16, verse 6. This probably conveyed to the first readers the idea that, although the boy had not died (Mark said he looked so much like a corpse that many said he was dead), what had happened to him was akin to a resurrection. That is, Mark is saying that the removal of the demon, a minion of Satan, is no less than bringing someone from death to life.

Further, the first readers, like us, may have seen an allusion to the death and resurrection of Jesus here. In death, Jesus would be seen as being trapped by Satan but, in the resurrection, he would be freed by another and able to stand again.

Healing through the prayer of faith (verses 28 and 29)

The ending Mark has given the story is reminiscent of the other times when Mark said Jesus gave private instruction to the disciples.[27] The theories have been almost endless as to what these passages mean. At least they mean that while those 'outside' may have misunderstood, the disciples had no excuse for not understanding. They had been privy to all that Jesus wanted to say.[28]

In turn, Mark is probably saying to his readers that they had no excuse for failing to understand, for he had made plain who Jesus is and what is required of his followers.

Jesus then explained why they had been unsuccessful in their attempt at an exorcism: 'This kind [of demon] can come out only through prayer.'[29]

The kind of demon thought to be involved was a 'dumb spirit'. Dumb spirits were considered particularly difficult to exorcise. Thus, the method of exorcism Mark is advocating for Christians is not the usual method of commanding a demon to depart, but the trusting prayer to God.[30]

From what Mark has said in this section on the importance of trust, prayer here would mean an expression of total trust in and dependence on the power and authority of the Holy Spirit given to the disciples by Jesus.

This understanding of prayer as involving trust was obviously important for Mark as he has spelt out the combination in chapter 11, verse 24: '. . .whatever you ask for in prayer, believe that you have received it, and it will be yours'.

Discussion questions

Talking it through

1 Why was Jesus upset with his disciples (verse 19)? Is it enough to say they did not have faith?

2 What does the father's reply in verse 24 tell us about faith? Is it encouraging? Disconcerting?

3 In what ways was Jesus' healing of the boy similar to a resurrection? Is this a useful way to think of it?

4 Bearing in mind Jesus' reply to the disciples in verse 29, what do you think prayer is?

Widening our horizons

1 Do you believe that situations exist today where exorcisms should take place? Is there any reason why you should not be used by God to carry out exorcisms? Do you see any dangers?

As a help in answering this, read the following:

Eventually, when the two were at a peak of animation, with flailing arms and flailing tongues, they finally seized on the liberation offered them by the simple words, 'choose God,' 'resist Satan' and the words of exorcism: 'In Jesus' name, leave them.'

We couldn't quite tell what was happening. We weren't using Jesus' name as a mantra, nor as a talisman. We said it because, quite simply, we meant it. We knew this was the way of performing exorcisms in the Bible; there seemed to be nothing else to say. But our hearers — or more precisely, their 'guests' — were wreathed in discomfort at Jesus' name. Wreathed, too, in resistance for minute after intense minute, until something snapped and in a roar that would freeze a tropical sunset, the resident spirits fled.'

(*New Internationalist*, November 1992)

2 What is faith? The following quotes might
help to clarify your thinking:
  (a) *Faith is a firm belief for which there is
      no evidence.*

                                    (Bertrand Russell)

  (b) *Seek not to understand that you may
      believe, but believe that you may
      understand.*

                                    (Saint Augustine)

  (c) *If we let ourselves believe. . . that man
      began with divine grace, that he forfeited this
      by sin, and that he can be redeemed only by
      divine grace through the crucified Christ, then
      we shall have a peace of mind never granted
      to philosophers.*

                                    (Blaise Pascal)

3 How can prayer be enhanced by the following:
  (a) kneeling?
  (b) hand movements?
  (c) eyes raised and open?
  (d) bodywork (e.g. beating the chest)?
      What does each pose indicate to you?
Why is this appropriate? How could each
be useful in producing an appropriate
attitude if we were seeking to be the
instrument of God's healing of someone?

5
Relationships
with others

What are some principles of
Christian community?

MARK CHAPTER 9, VERSES 30 TO 42

THE JOURNEY CONTINUES. In saying that the disciples 'passed through Galilee' (verse 30), Mark
shows that the Galilean ministry of miracles and
public teaching has finished. This had culminated
at Caesarea Philippi where, at the northern-most
point of Jesus' travels, Peter had made his famous
declaration: 'You are the Messiah.' Now begins the
decisive movement south — towards Jerusalem.
(From the parallel passage in chapter 10, verse 32,
we see that the holy city was the destination.)

Jesus again foretells his suffering (verses 30 to 32)

Why did Jesus hide his whereabouts? It is incomprehensible to think that in saying he 'did not want anyone to know it' (verse 30), Mark meant Jesus wanted to avoid detection and arrest by the authorities.[1] Mark goes on to show that Jesus' destiny is to be in the hands of *God*, not people.

Rather, as verse 31 explains, there were still things Jesus wanted to teach his disciples. In other words, the image of a triumphant and all-powerful Jesus, so far revealed in Mark's story, is an incomplete, distorted one without the story of his suffering, death and resurrection.

For a second time, then, Jesus teaches his disciples: 'The Son of Man is to be betrayed into human hands, and they will kill him, and three days after being killed, he will rise again' (verse 31). In using the imperfect tense 'he taught' (*edidasken*), which indicates an ongoing action, Mark may be saying that Jesus was repeatedly teaching his disciples about his ignominious end. This is all the more likely when we note that Mark records Jesus predicting his suffering and death three times.

A most significant feature of this prediction in verse 31 is the use of the word 'to betray' (*paradidonai*) for what was to happen to Jesus.[2] It is a word with a wide range of meanings, including 'ready to be picked',[3] 'handing on a tradition',[4] 'giving up one's life, handing over someone for punishment',[5] — as well as 'betraying someone to any enemy'.[6]

It is probable that those who first read Mark would have understood two things by this word. First, they would naturally have had *Judas* in mind, for Mark uses the words 'deliver' or 'betrayer' many times for Judas and his act.[7] Second, Mark's readers may have understood that *God*, who was in control of Jesus' life and was perhaps to be contrasted with the 'human hands' of this verse, was the one willing to 'hand over' his Son to be killed.[8]

The play on words between 'Son of Man' and '*human* hands' highlights this contrast. The passive tense of 'betray' or 'hand over' may be a translation of a Semitic idiom which would also have carried connotations of God being involved in the handing over of Jesus to human hands. Also, this idea becomes even more plausible when we recognise that, at the time, it was a word in Jewish writings used of God allowing or stopping the handing over of a martyr to be killed.[9]

Yet again the disciples are said not to understand. That the chosen Messiah and glorious Son of Man should need to suffer and die before being raised to honour is, not surprisingly, initially incomprehensible to human minds.

But why should Mark say that the disciples, as well as not comprehending, were also 'afraid to ask'

Jesus? Could it be that the disciples feared the same fate? It was well recognised that the fate of a leader was a model for his followers. This is likely to be Mark's view, for what follows in this section of his Gospel, as well as the teaching that has gone before, focuses on the suffering that is integral to being a follower of Jesus.

Christian community (verses 33 to 37)

The house referred to is probably intended to be Peter's home.[10] That the setting for this section of teaching (up to chapter 9, verse 50) was the home of the 'great' Peter (who may have been especially important to Mark's readers) may have signalled to the readers the special significance of what they were about to read or hear.[11]

Mark has been depicting the disciples as walking on their journey with Jesus, which we could assume means he would have heard everything they said. So, it comes as a surprise for us to hear Jesus ask his disciples what they were arguing about on the way.[12]

However, according to the conventions regarding the conduct of relationships between a teacher and his pupils, a disciple had to walk behind — he was not permitted to walk alongside his master.[13] We see this in chapter 10, verse 32 where, according to this convention, Mark says that Jesus was walking ahead of disciples on the way to Jerusalem. Thus, as Jesus would have been thought to be walking ahead of his disciples on the way into Capernaum, he could quite reasonably be expected to ask about the subject of an argument he heard on the way.

❏ *Who is the greatest? (verse 34)*
This is the only time Mark portrays the disciples as arguing amongst themselves. As the group of disciples represents the Christian community, Mark is probably affirming that the basic issue in the Christian community is 'Who is the greatest?' Mark's use of the present tense in verse 35 may further confirm that Mark's readers would see the question as having ongoing significance for them.

That the disciples are said to be arguing 'on the way' — which for Mark, is a phrase encapsulating the Christian life of following Jesus — heightens the tragedy of the nature of the argument. Dietrich Bonhoeffer affirms this:

> No Christian community ever comes together without this thought immediately emerging as a seed of discord. Thus at the very beginning of Christian fellowship there is engendered an invisible, often unconscious, life-and-death contest. . . This is enough to destroy a fellowship.[14]

Then he says:

> All this can occur in the most polite or even pious environment. . . It is the struggle of the

natural man for self-justification. He finds it only in comparing himself with others, in condemning and judging others.[15]

❏ *Principles for good Christian relationships (verses 35 to 37)*

Last time Mark reported Jesus predicting his suffering and death. The issue he connected with it for the disciples was that of self-denial and taking up one's cross. Here it is the issue of internal relations in the community.

That Jesus should be said to sit down in verse 35, just like a rabbi, suggests that he is about to deliver some important teaching.[16] This idea is reinforced by Mark — he stresses that the teaching is for the followers of Jesus by unnecessarily saying that Jesus 'called the Twelve', for they are already with him.[17]

(a) The first principle of good relationships (verse 35)

The key principle on how relationships are to function among followers of Jesus is: 'Whoever wants to be first must be last of all and servant of all' (verse 35). As we will see, Mark considers this principle to be so important he repeats it with variations on two further occasions.[18] At this point the principle requires a number of comments.

* Mark is probably dealing with the issue of leadership rather than simple importance or significance.

In chapter 6, verse 21, he uses the word 'first'
(*prōtos*) of political leaders and, here, the antithesis
of first or leader is servant.[19]

* This saying assumes that in the church — as in
  any human organisation — there is the need for
  those who are leaders and those who are led.
  Therefore, this saying cannot be used to support
  the view that Jesus did away with rank in the
  Christian community. The assumption of the existence of rank is an interesting point worth
  pondering for contemporary Western Christians.
  I believe it is an illusion to use Mark 9, verse 35
  as a basis for treating church leaders as merely
  figureheads.
* 'Whoever wants to be first' recognises that some
  members of the Christian community desire to
  be leaders. It is notable that this desire is not
  here questioned as wrong. What is questioned
  is *how* the leadership is to be obtained and main-
  tained.
* The saying goes on to spell out that Christian
  leadership is attained by being 'last of all'.

When dealing with the implication of discipleship
in relationship to Jesus, the issue and principle was
of self-denial, of saying 'no' to oneself. When intro-
ducing that principle, Mark uses the introductory
phrase, 'Whoever wishes' (*ei tis thelei*). Now, in
chapter 9, verse 35, using exactly the same wording,

precisely the same principle is introduced and paralleled.

In relation to others, a Christian leader is also to deny himself. In this way, the principle of self-glory and self-attainment, so readily acknowledged in the world, is completely reversed. In the context of this passage, Mark is redirecting both the thoughts of their own glory and the means of attaining it away from selfish ends to the need to suffer. That is the means to glory. This principle is entirely in keeping with that which Mark says governed Jesus' leadership of the disciples — and therefore of the Christian church to which he is speaking.[20]

(b) The second principle of good relationships (verse 35)
It is possible that the parallelism in the Greek of chapter 9, verse 35 — 'last of all' and 'servant of all' — means that the phrases are to be taken together as saying the same thing. However, to elucidate all that Mark is trying to say about relationships in the Christian community we will take them separately. The principle that whoever wishes to be first or a leader must be 'servant of all' merits a number of comments:

* To serve or be a servant was not considered to be a pleasant role in Mark's world. So for Greek readers, a 'servant' (*diakonos*) waited on tables and looked after the general needs of a household. Not surprisingly, this personal subjection was not

considered worthy of a free person; the giving of oneself in the service of others was alien to Greeks. The personal goal of a human being was not servitude, but the development of his own personality. Mark's readers may well have known that the Latin cognate for the Greek *diakoneō* was *conari*, which meant 'to give oneself trouble'!

Josephus the historian, who was writing about the same time as Mark, said that his fellow Jews, the Essenes, did not wish to have servants, but to care for each other.[21] However, by and large amongst Jews at the time, it was unusual for significant people to wait on tables.[22] Such service was beneath the dignity of a free person.[23] Instead, social responsibility for the poor was carried out through the regular Friday collection and distribution of food.[24]

* For Mark to be telling his readers that a key principle of the relationship of a leader to his or her people was one of service would have been recognised as an unpleasant reversal of the generally acceptable principles of community relationships and human dignity.

* The suffering is not proposed for any self-centred purpose such as character-building.[25] Rather, the suffering of servitude is directed towards the well-being of those being led. This is a principle widely recognised in the early church, even after

the time of Mark.

✳ We cannot conclude from this principle that the group is the master of the leader. This distorted principle is well expressed by the television character, Prime Minister Jim Hacker: 'The people have spoken, I am their leader, I must follow.'

The only master recognised by Mark is Jesus. To quote Bonheoffer again:

Strong and weak, wise and foolish, gifted or ungifted, pious or impious, the diverse individuals in the community are no longer incentives for talking and judging and condemning, and thus excuses for self-justification. They are rather cause for rejoicing in one another and serving one another. Each member of the community is given his particular place, but this is no longer the place in which he can most successfully assert himself, but the place where he can perform his service.[26]

(c) The third principle of good relationships (verse 37)
We need to be careful in our interpretation of this principle. One suggestion is that Mark is using this saying to teach his readers how to be hospitable to travelling missionaries. Even though Mark has taken up the theme earlier,[27] it is unlikely to be part of his intention here, for the context tells us he is dealing with internal relations within a Christian community. How Christians should treat members

of other churches is dealt with in the next paragraph of Mark.

For Mark, as for earlier Greeks, a 'child' (*paidion*) referred to someone up to the age of seven.[28] Interestingly, in the Greek Bible, the Septuagint (LXX), the word was used to illustrate a child's capacity for being a companion, a messenger and a servant.[29]

Also, before looking more directly at the saying, we should note that in the ancient world of Mark's readers it was the mature, healthy adult who was the ideal human. In contrast to contemporary Western thinking, which has idealised the child of good health and innocence, in the ancient world the child was a person of unimportance, need and dependence. For example, in Jewish thinking, a boy did not count as a person until he was old enough to become a child of the law.[30]

Therefore, in being told to welcome a child, Jesus was not saying that a disciple should become like a child in either trust or innocence. (That lesson will come in chapter 10, verse 15.) Rather, to welcome a child was to take note of and care for the unimportant, needy and dependent in the Christian community.

To 'welcome' (*dechomai*) someone was not simply to offer someone hospitality,[31] as it may mean for a contemporary Western Christian. To welcome someone implied an intimate acceptance of that person — like taking a child into one's arms, as it does here.[32]

So, according to this principle of relationships in the Christian community, whoever wishes to welcome or receive Jesus — making him the centre of attention in his or her life — must welcome or intimately receive the unimportant, needy and dependent in the Christian community. In short, to be a follower of Jesus is to imitate him in intimately receiving the weaker and less important brothers and sisters.

How to treat different kinds of Christians (verses 38 to 42)

Mark now moves from principles about how Christians are to treat each other in their churches to setting some principles on how whole groups of Christians should treat each other.

❏ *The strange exorcist*

The very brief story of the so-called 'strange exorcist' is full of interest. It probably tells us that Jesus was such a successful and powerful exorcist that his fellow Jews quickly took up using his name as part of their repertoire of powerful names.[33] The story also probably tells us that Jesus did not think he was the only effective Jewish exorcist of his time.

This tiny story tells us that early Christians performed exorcisms in 'the name of Jesus'. The name of someone was thought to represent them — its utterance to carry with it the power of the person's presence. Hence, to use the name of Jesus in exorcism would have been to say something like, 'in the name of Jesus, I command you to come out', as the sons of Sceva did in Acts 19, verse 13. This was seen as the equivalent of the person whose powerful name was being used being present.

❏ *The stranger*
More importantly, Mark's readers would probably see the story as reflecting their own desire to exclude any Christian who was not a member of their community. The fact that the saying mentions following 'us' rather than 'you' would also alert Mark's readers to the ongoing relevance of the story.

That the strange exorcist represents other Christians or people about to become Christians rather than non-Christians using the name of Jesus seems probable from the verses immediately preceding this, where there was discussion about Christians relating to each other,[34] and especially chapter 9, verse 42 which suggests that Christians have been the subject of the passage in hand.

Jesus replied to John: 'Do not stop him; for no-one who does a deed of power in my name will be able soon afterward to speak evil of me' (verse 39). From the perspective of the first readers, this would mean that the person represented by the strange exorcist was, if not a Christian, on the way to becoming one.

Keeping in mind the immediately preceding theme of the servant attitude required of those wishing to be leaders, this story would also be a direction for them to be prepared to include those on the way to becoming a Christian. Verse 40 ('Whoever is not against us is for us') makes this point. Further, verse 41 confirms and widens this perspective. It shows that not only those involved in the ministry of exorcism, but also those seeking to enter into the task of caring for Christians will be rewarded.

In a harsh hot climate, familiar to people of the Mediterranean, the giving of a cup of water would have been a symbol of kind hospitality. The ones offering this hospitality to those who 'bear the name of Christ' are clearly meant to be those outsiders about to become Christians, not only because of their interest in entering into the task of caring for Christians, but because it is said that 'they will by no means lose the reward'.

The word 'reward' (*misthos*) is only used here in verse 41 in Mark. From the immediate context as well as its use in similar ways in other places, it is clearly the 'reward of salvation'.[35] We should not think for a moment that the reward is something deserved. The idea is quite foreign to the teaching of Jesus and the New Testament.[36] The idea of a deserved reward for moral action is also foreign to this passage where, otherwise, salvation would be rewarded on the basis of giving a single glass of water. Rather, this verse simply talks about those acting kindly to Christians, who are themselves on the way to becoming Christians. They are not to be excluded, for God is aware of them.

Indeed, so serious is the matter of causing Christians to stumble, that it would (according to verse 42) be better for the person to have a great millstone hung around his or her neck and thrown into the sea.

The 'little ones' are Christians, for they are said to believe in Jesus.[37] The 'great' (onikos) millstone is not the small hand-turned mill used by women, but the stone so large that it required a donkey (onikos) to turn it. The severity and reality of this punishment for someone deflecting another's trust in Christ would have been graphic at a time when drowning was a form of capital punishment.[38]

Discussion questions

Talking it through

1 How does the word 'betrayed' in verse 31, with its multi-layered meaning, bring out the horror of Jesus' suffering?

2 The term 'servant leadership' claims to reflect the principle in verse 35. Does it? What do you understand by the term?

3 What attitude to hospitality is being advocated in verse 37?

4 What group of people should we accept in verses 38 to 42? What evidence is there for this?

5 Reading between the lines a little, what can we learn about the Christian community Mark was writing for from chapter 9, verses 33 to 42?

Widening our horizons

1 How can each of the following institutions reflect Jesus' model of relationships outlined in verse 35:
(a) the church?
(b) the family?
(c) the workplace?
(d) the government?
   What model do each of these reflect in your experience? What changes are desirable? How can they be made?

2 What following models of child-rearing do you see as reflecting the pattern Jesus lays down in verse 37:
(a) shaping the child in the parents' mould?
(b) encouraging the child to develop his individuality, even if that is different from the parent?

3 Do you believe you should provide hospitality for each of the following:
(a) a homeless person for the night?
(b) a group of teenagers wanting to sleep

over for the night?

(c) an adult child indefinitely?

(d) an aging relative unable to care for herself on a permanent basis?

If you believe support should be given, what conditions should apply that would not detract from the welcome? What about irreconcilable differences?

4 How can we encourage the common bonds between:

(a) those committed to Jesus and those 'on the way' to commitment?

(b) those of different denominations?

(c) those of different theological persuasion?

To what extent do you see the stumbling blocks as theological and to what extent do you think they are sociological and psychological?

6
Lessons for disciples

How should followers of Jesus live?
MARK CHAPTER 9, VERSE 43 TO
CHAPTER 10, VERSE 16

IN THE LAST CHAPTER WE SAW MARK dealing with
the rightful demands of Christians on other followers
of Jesus. Nothing was to be done which would
cause another Christian to stumble (*skandalizō*).
Now, through a series of sayings he has collected
together, Mark turns to deal with what Jesus requires
in the life of any one of his followers so they do not
stumble, but remain faithful.

It is quite possible that Mark, or an earlier Christian, linked these sayings together through a series
of catch words and phrases: for example, my name
— your name — my name — Christ's name — to

stumble — better — to stumble — better — to
stumble — better — to stumble — better — fire —
salted — fire — salted — good. This would help
young Christians memorise the teaching of Jesus.

The cost of obedience
(chapter 9, verses 43 to 48)
To begin, Mark gives his readers three graphic
sayings of Jesus which show starkly the importance
and the cost of 'entering life'. But first, a study of
some key words.

❏ *A word study of four key words*
In order to understand these sayings, there are four
recurring words or phrases which it helps to understand:

(a) 'Stumble' (skandalizō). Basically, the word meant
'trap.'[1] It came from *skandalon* which was that part
of a trap on which the bait was put. So 'stumble'
came to mean 'to lead away', or 'to provoke or trap
someone in sin'.[2] Just once, in chapter 6, verse 3,
Mark uses the word for causing offence.

Importantly for our understanding of Mark,
'stumble' came to mean 'to apostatise' or 'give up
belief' as it most naturally does in Mark.[3] So the
issue at stake in these verses is one's own trust in
Christ.

(b) 'Life' (*zoē*). Does Mark mean eternal life experienced in this life, or does he mean eternal life in the age to come, as in chapter 10, verse 30? It seems that Mark has in mind the latter, for he contrasts it with being thrown into the unquenchable fire of hell (see below). However, in verse 47, he substitutes 'kingdom of God' for 'life' in the two earlier sayings.[4] Therefore, this apparently obvious meaning will need some modification.

(c) 'Kingdom of God' (*basileia tou theou*). This is the second time in the chapters of the book treated in this commentary that Mark has used the phrase 'kingdom of God'. He will use it five more times in the material we will cover.[5] As important as the term is for Mark, he uses it far less than Matthew and Luke.[6]

One of our great difficulties in understanding the term is that it has meant slightly different things to different people: the Old Testament writers, Jews around the time of Jesus, Jesus himself as well as the Gospel writers, and people in the twentieth century. Our task is to try to discover what Mark and his readers understood by the phrase.

Mark first uses 'the kingdom of God' in chapter 1, verse 15 where it is a synonym for the gospel or good news which Jesus preaches. There, Mark is saying that through God's initiative the 'decisive appointed time' (*kairos*) has 'come to fulfilment', yet it also has ongoing implications (*peplērōtai*). At a point where we might wish otherwise, Mark has been ambiguous in saying that either the kingdom of God has 'come near' or has 'arrived' (*engizein*). From what Mark says later, this ambiguity is intentional. While the coming of Jesus means that God's reign had arrived in history,[7] it is still, to some extent, hidden and awaiting complete appearance.[8]

Thus, we can return to the question of the meaning of 'life' in chapter 9, verses 43 and 45. In being contrasted with hell, it clearly means primarily the future eternal life. In being a synonym for 'kingdom of God', Mark has in mind the experience of God's reign here and now.

(d) 'Hell' (*geenna*). This is the only place in Mark where the word is used so, apart from the background to the word, we are limited to the context of what he says here for its precise meaning.

The word he uses is *geenna*, transliterated as 'Gehenna'. In turn, it comes from the Hebrew *gehinnom*, meaning 'valley of Hinnom'. This was the valley running around the south-west corner of Jerusalem. In early times, the valley was a place where infants were sacrificed to Molech.[9] Later, it was desecrated by Josiah and became the site for burning offal.[10] By the time of Jesus and the New Testament writers, the Hinnom valley was a symbol of future punishment.[11]

The Hebrew loan-word from Palestine, Gehenna,

was probably unintelligible to readers in Rome. Therefore, the first time Mark used the word, he added an explanatory phrase in verse 48, 'where their worm never dies, and the fire is never quenched'. This phrase is probably dependent on Isaiah 66, verse 24. (A more obvious paraphrase of this verse is in verse 48 of this chapter.) In this way, Mark explained to his readers that Gehenna was the place of future destruction and abandonment for those who rebelled against God.

❏ *How valuable is the Christian life?*
  (verses 43 to 48)

The three sayings about the hand, foot and eye convey the same teaching, but each has its own distinctive nuance. Each saying says that it is better to enter life without a particular part of one's body than to go to hell with a complete body.

(a) Worth more than a hand (verse 43). Of all the parts of the body, for the Greeks the hand was seen as the most used. To mention a person's hand could be to mention his or her activities; the hand could be referred to in order to represent a person's power and authority.

Thus, in the Old Testament, a person's activity was said to be the work of his or her hand.[12] Therefore, according to this verse, if a person's activity or work was trapping them into losing their trust in Jesus, it was worth losing everything rather than going to hell.

(b) Worth more than a foot (verse 45). In the Old Testament, the foot is used metaphorically at least forty times to represent a person. If a distinction is possible between the metaphorical use of hand and foot, it is that, whereas the hand represented the work or activity of a person, the foot represented direction, disposition or purpose of one's life. Through reference to the foot, a person could be said to be resting or restless,[13] to be consecrated to something or to be victorious over an enemy.[14]

Thus, by referring to one's foot, Mark may be intending the readers to understand that one's life values and directions could cause a person to fall away from a life of trust in Christ.

(c) Worth more than an eye (verse 47). In Mark's thought-world, the eye was the principal organ of perception and contact with the world. More particularly, for the New Testament writers, the eye was associated with moral concepts and was the organ of understanding and knowing. Not surprisingly, it was the most valued organ of the body.[15] Thus, the injunction to tear out one's eye rather than be thrown into hell could be taken not only to mean that one's moral and intellectual choices should not be allowed to cause one to lose trust in Christ, but that even the most valuable things should not be permitted to cause one to stumble.

Therefore, as a series, the three sayings may be designed to reach a climax — to drive home the point that nothing in a person's life should be allowed to impede one's trust in Christ. Put another way, it is worth sacrificing everything to maintain one's trust in Christ. The alternative is too dreadful to contemplate.

Clearly, these sayings are a present warning to followers of Jesus on how they are to live, rather than an attempt to provide teaching on future rewards and punishments. While we may learn something about future punishment, to take these sayings as other than warnings is to fail to be prepared to live in submissive trust to him.

Sayings on salt (chapter 9, verses 49 and 50)

It is the view of virtually all students of the New Testament that Mark, or perhaps those from whom he received the traditions about Jesus, collected together these sayings on salt. They were probably placed here because 'fire' (*pur*) could be used as a link word. Regardless of this, we must try to discover what Mark meant by them to begin with.

Because of their context and the disciples being the audience, they clearly have to do with discipleship.[16] As there have been very many quite different suggestions as to the meaning of these verses, we are cautioned from being dogmatic.

For Mark as well as other New Testament writers, 'for' (*gar*) usually connects a passage to what precedes it. If that is Mark's intention here (in verse

49), then the fire of salt is to be connected with the fire of judgment in verses 43 to 48. However, to say that everyone will be salted with or experience the fire of judgment contradicts the clear option in verses 43 to 48 of avoiding judgment. Therefore, the connection between these verses and what goes before is to be found in the catch-word 'fire'. In turn, the word 'salt' rather than a particular theme connects verse 49 to verse 50.

❏ *The salt of suffering (verse 49)*
Apart from the story of the demon-possessed boy, where the fire referred to is a literal, (probably) cooking fire (chapter 9, verse 22), this is the only section in which 'fire' (*pur*) is used by Mark.[17] Among the early Christians, 'fire' often had the meaning of suffering or 'persecution'.[18]

If 'salt' is given the meaning of 'purify', verse 49 would mean that every disciple will be purified by suffering or persecution. If Mark was written at the end of the 60s in Rome, such an interpretation of this verse is credible.

❏ *The irreplaceable salt (verse 50)*
However, in the first part of verse 50, the meaning of salt is most probably different. It could be that the salt is the essence of being a Christian. This would then mean that if a Christian has lost his trust in Jesus — that which makes a person a disciple — it is an unanswerable question as to what can help

the person. This interpretation holds good for the middle part of verse 50 with its direction to have salt in or within yourselves.

The final portion of the verse — 'and be at peace with one another' — recalls the theme of this section of Mark which extends back to chapter 9, verse 33 and draws it to a close. Integral to Christian discipleship is not only an individual following of Jesus, which has been the focus of the immediately preceding material but, as this phrase reiterates, a humble cooperation with each other.

Lessons on marriage and divorce (Chapter 10, verses 1 to 12)

In our time, the understanding of marriage has undergone a revolution. *Newsweek* some time ago reported that in Scandinavia, more and more young couples are avoiding marriage. One man, living with his girlfriend, was cited as saying: 'Marriage as an institution doesn't really mean anything anymore.' In Sweden and Iceland, half the children are now born to unmarried women. Many who do marry do not see the relationship as an exclusive lifelong commitment.

A survey in Australia suggests that about half of all husbands will have affairs at some stage in their marriages.[19] Further, in recent years, divorce rates have been astronomically high. The Australian Bureau of Statistics depicts the typical Australian divorcee as in their 30s, married for ten years and having two dependent children. Also, the bureau has estimated that about one in five of the couples married ten years ago are now divorced. Divorce is even common among Christians, as is remarriage.

❑ *The background*
In the first century, divorce was also common. We have little information about Greco-Roman laws under which Mark's readers in Rome lived. However, divorce seems to have been easily obtained by either partner. Those of Mark's readers who were Jews had the prescription set out in Deuteronomy 24, verse 1:

> Suppose a man enters into marriage with a woman, but she does not please him because he finds something objectionable about her, and so he writes her a certificate of divorce, puts it in her hand and sends her out of his house.

For some Jews, like Rabbi Shammai, this meant that only unchastity was a ground for divorce. But for others, like Hillel the Elder, even a spoiled meal was grounds for divorce. Another rabbi taught that a man could divorce his wife for a prettier woman.[20] Also, Josephus divorced his wife, 'being displeased at her behaviour'.[21]

The document of divorce, signed by two witnesses, appears to be no more than the husband declaring his wife is free to remarry.[22] Such a view was based on a generally low view of women. For example, Josephus said: 'In every respect, women are subordinate to men.'[23] And, twice daily, devout Jewish men prayed: 'Blessed are you who did not make me a. . . woman.' Nevertheless, if a man was unable to fulfil his marital obligations or was loathsome to his wife, she could apply to the courts for a divorce.[24]

It is against this sexually permissive background that Mark sets out the rigorous Christian teaching on marriage and divorce.

The strictness and difficulty of the teaching is reinforced by its setting. In chapter 10, verse 1, Mark has Jesus leave Galilee and move towards Jerusalem, the place of his imminent suffering and death. The disciples and those who wished to become followers of Jesus had already learnt that discipleship meant saying 'no' to oneself and taking up their cross (chapter 8, verse 34). Now, Mark shows the crowds listening to the teaching of Jesus to discover the cost involved in being one of his followers.

Those contemplating becoming followers of Jesus were to discover that the Hellenistic and Jewish views on marriage and divorce would have to be abandoned.

❑ *Is divorce lawful? (verses 1 to 9)*
The Pharisees, one of the antagonists in Mark's story,

questioned Jesus: 'Is it lawful for a man to divorce his wife?' They came not seeking teaching, but in the hope of getting him to say something which they could use against him.

Jewish readers of Mark would have been keen to know if the Christian view of marriage and divorce followed the strict Shammai or more liberal Hillel school. Instead, the Pharisees are taken back to the Law: 'What did Moses command you?' (verse 3). In answer, the Pharisees cited not a command, but a place in the books of Moses where divorce is regularised, rather than judged one way or the other.

In turn, Jesus made a distinction between Moses permitting divorce because of 'your hardness of heart' or rebellion against God (*sklērokardian*: verse 5) and what God actually intended. To do this, Jesus directed attention to Genesis 1, verse 27 and chapter 2, verse 24 as expressing God's original intention for marriage.

Jesus said that these verses in Genesis show God's intention in creating man and woman was that, in marriage, the two should become an indissoluble one. From this Jesus drew the conclusion that divorce is not permitted: '. . .what God has joined together, let no-one separate' (Mark 10, verse 9).

Clearly, Mark's readers were to understand that to be involved in divorce would be to come under the judgment of God.

❑ *Further clarification (verses 10 to 12)*
Elsewhere, Mark depicts the disciples as receiving private teaching, in order to explain previous teaching.[25] Here the disciples asked about this severe statement on the indissolubility of marriage, presumably to get more detail.

According to Jewish law, a man has wronged the husband of the woman with whom he has committed adultery, not the woman herself. So Jesus' statement here that 'Whoever divorces his wife and marries another commits adultery against *her*' (chapter 10, verse 11) goes beyond and is much more severe than Mark's Jewish readers may have expected.

Different Jewish communities may have had different regulations regarding the wife's ability to divorce her husband. In the Jewish community at Elephantine on the Nile, a woman could divorce her husband.[26] Also, by the second century AD in Palestine, a wife could petition the courts for a divorce.[27]

However, Mark says that Jesus taught that such an action on the part of the wife is committing adultery. In short, marriage is a lifelong union created by God. Any attempt to breach this relationship is to come under the judgment of God.

A lesson on attitudes (chapter 10, verses 13 to 16)

At first glance it appears that Mark is dealing with

family issues: first marriage and divorce, and then children. However, a more careful examination of what he has written shows that Mark continues to deal with issues and lessons on discipleship, in this case the child-like attitudes required of a follower of Jesus.

Someone has said: 'The thing that impresses me most about America is the way parents obey their children.' The same could be said of British, New Zealand and Australian parents. We idolise the fresh vitality and innocence of our children, too often believing that their demands are their rights.

Not so in the world of Jesus and the first readers of Mark. Children were easily ignored and thought to be unimportant. It was the fit and fully developed adult who was the epitome of humanity.[28] It is not surprising, then, for the disciples to be shown to be speaking sternly to those bothering Jesus with children.

❑ A reference to baptism?

This passage has often been used to justify the practice of the baptism of infants.[29] For example, as early as the writing of Justin Martyr,[30] the passage was understood to refer to baptism. However, the important question is whether or not Mark intended his readers to take it this way. Also, the reference to 'not forbidding' the children to come to Jesus could, some think, refer to early church hindrances to baptism. But, again, it would need to be demonstrated that Mark had this idea in mind.

The laying-on of hands has also been seen to be an indication that this passage has to do with baptism. On the other hand, the laying-on of hands need be no more than a sign of blessing.[31] Further, in Mark's story of the baptism of Jesus (chapter 1 verses 9 to 11), the laying-on of hands plays no part.[32]

Apart from these points, there are good reasons for rejecting any reference to baptism in this passage.

First, the part of Mark's Gospel dealt with in this book deals with the demands of discipleship. It would be incongruous for Mark to insert a passage in which he is saying, 'Being a follower of Jesus means bringing your children for baptism.'[33]

Second, a careful look at what Mark is saying in this passage shows that he is not dealing with baptism, nor even with the problem of children joining the church. Rather, in using the words 'such as' (verse 14) and 'as' (verse 15), Mark is clearly portraying the child as a model.

It cannot be that the child *is* a model of the kingdom for, as we have seen, children were not highly regarded, and receiving them would not reflect the honour and respect with which the kingdom is to be received. Nor, indeed, did Matthew understand the child as a model of the kingdom of God.[34] It is not even Mark's intention that discipleship involves treating others as Jesus treats children. Verse 15 excludes such a view.

❏ *A model disciple*

The most natural reading of our passage is that a child is a model disciple in the way it receives the kingdom of God. The implication of this is well explained by Ernest Best:

> A child trusts adults: he has confidence in them; he receives from them what they offer. So the disciple is to trust God and receive the kingdom. The kingdom is not a place or a thing; it is God's active rule; the disciple has therefore to allow God to rule in his life. This is not something which is completed once and for all in the act of becoming a disciple, but something which takes place continuously. . .[35]

Discussion questions

Talking it through

1 What ideas lie behind the term 'kingdom of God' in this passage? How could this phrase be translated for us today?

2 What does discipleship mean to Jesus, according to verses 43 to 48? If verse 49 is taken into account, is there comfort in these verses?

3 How is verse 50 relevant to this view: 'I don't believe that Jesus is who the Bible claims he is, but I follow his moral teachings — in that sense I am a disciple.'

4 How is Jesus' teaching on marriage and divorce linked with discipleship? What is the core concept common to both?

5 Why are children used in verse 15 as examples of discipleship? What does Jesus want us to learn from them?

Widening our horizons

1 How do you understand eternity? In your answer, take into account some or all of the following:
   (a) where heaven is located
   (b) what hell is
   (c) what judgment means
   (d) whether the common expressions 'heaven on earth' or 'hell on earth' are related to eternity
   (e) what you see as the very essence of heaven (as distinct from detail).
      How important is eternal life to you?

2 Recent research in many Western countries suggests that the percentage of the population that believe marriage is for life is growing and that support for it as a lifelong commitment is highest in the teenage and early twenties group.
   Can you offer any explanation for this pattern? How do you think we might nurture this idealism in young people?

3 Jesus emphasises the *difficulty* of following him, whereas most politicians emphasise how everything will be *easier* if you follow them. Which approach:

(a) is likely to win more support?

(b) is likely to produce more lasting results?

How far does history support your conclusions?

4 Women were one of many repressed groups Jesus stood by. How do you imagine Jesus would handle each of the following today:

(a) wives battered by their husbands?

(b) prisoners subjected to rape?

(c) minority ethnic groups suppressed by their governments?

Is this way of looking at current conflicts helpful? What ways other than the aggressor-victim model can we use?

5 Does everything that the church does need to have biblical backing? If not, why is there so much stress on finding a biblical basis for each of the following:

(a) the form of baptism?

(b) the form of church government?

(c) the form of the Eucharist/Lord's Supper/Holy Communion?

7
Wealth and materialism

Is this the hardest lesson?
MARK CHAPTER 10, VERSES 17 TO 31

IT IS NOT SEX OR DRUGS OR ALCOHOL which are stumbling blocks to discipleship in the Western world; it is the pursuit of wealth and materialism.

Would-be followers of Jesus can rightly claim, at least superficially, to have kept the Ten Commandments. Yet, the desire for personal pleasure through acquiring extra or better cars, video machines, a country retreat, a secure retirement or better furniture and clothes has diverted the great mass of Christians in our cultures from obeying the call of Jesus to be his followers. I believe that such money-centred activities as pressurising children to earn money while studying and so jeopardising that study, and seeking overtime and financial success at work have done more to damage true discipleship than any other single factor amongst Western Christians.

It is no wonder that this section of Mark on wealth and materialism is either rarely studied in Christian circles or is reinterpreted to make it comfortable for Christians to remain greedy.

The rich man with everything yet nothing (verses 17 to 22)

The approach of the man in verse 17 to Jesus — perhaps intended as a representative for those in his situation — is couched in terms of reverence and respect. He kneels and addresses Jesus as 'Good Teacher', a rarely used address of flattery.[1] Indeed, as Jesus goes on to point out: 'No-one is good but God alone' (verse 18). For, even though people were sometimes called 'good' in the Old Testament,[2] only God is generally described as 'good'.[3]

The reverent words of the man are in keeping with his actions: he has been expecting his own goodness and reverence to contribute or help him gain eternal life. For, in Psalm 15, the question of who may live in the company of God is answered by reference to living as the law commands. Yet the question, 'What must I do to inherit eternal life?' and the ensuing dialogue show that the man recognises that his reverence for God and keeping the law cannot assure him of eternal life. In the question, the use of the word 'inherit', with its strong Old Testament background, shows that the man understood that eternal life is not obtained through a transaction with God, but received as a gracious gift from him.[4]

Probably too much has been made of Jesus saying, 'Why do you call me good? No-one is good but God alone' (verse 18). Some, like Saint Ambrose of Milan in the fourth century, have thought that Jesus is correcting the man so that he can recognise the divinity of Jesus.[5] Others have seen the statement as an admission of imperfection. However, in the light of the rest of Mark, it is more reasonable to see Mark as conveying to his readers that God is seen in Jesus because Jesus seeks nothing for himself. Rather, Jesus directs his attention and that of those who follow him to God alone.

Mark does not want us to think that the man is boasting when he tells Jesus that he has kept all the law since his youth (verse 20). Mark immediately affirms the man's life by saying that Jesus loved him (verse 21). Also, Jesus' statement to the rich man shows that he has done everything except one thing — follow Jesus. It is in following Jesus that eternal life is received.

❏ *Saying 'No' to wealth*
Jesus said, 'You lack one thing; go, sell what you own, and give the money to the poor, and you will

have treasure in heaven; then come, follow me'
(verse 21). So far in Mark's Gospel, those who have
become followers of Jesus have been depicted as
leaving fishing, family and tax collecting.[6]

It is clear in these cases that the acts of leaving
or renunciation are not legalistic acts of achievement
required to be fulfilled in order to be a follower of
Jesus. Rather, they are things left aside as a conse-
quence of responding to the call of Jesus to be his
follower. Thus, it is not likely that Jesus requires a
further law to be fulfilled before the rich man can
be accepted as a follower.

❏ *Obedience or giving?*
When so many Western Christians see giving to the
poor as an essential part of being a follower of Jesus,
it is to be noted that the command to give to the
poor is probably not the key element of what Mark
had in mind here. It is not even that every follower
of Jesus must leave family and possessions and
travel with Jesus. In the story of the Gadarene
demoniac, for instance, Jesus told the healed man
'to go home to his friends'.[7] What Jesus requires,
according to Mark, is total obedience in which nothing is to hinder being one of his followers. So, in
becoming one of his followers, some will have to
leave behind family and some will have to leave
behind possessions.[8] We will see more of this
towards the end of this chapter.

❏ *Grief-stricken*
On hearing Jesus' demand, the would-be follower is
said to have become 'gloomy' or 'shocked' (*stug-
nazein*). How he felt is described by the word
lupoumenos; he was 'grieving'. He grieves, 'for he
had many possessions' (verse 22). The word
'possession' (*ktēma*) is not simply money. It is used
for landed property: a farm or an estate.

It has been noted before that this is the only
person in the Gospel stories who is said to leave the
presence of Jesus grieving. Also, this man is the
only person in the stories of the Gospels who refuses
the call to follow Jesus. We can note again that
this is a clear indication that Mark probably considered wealth and materialism to be the greatest
threat to a person's being able to follow Jesus.

The problem of wealth
(verses 23 to 27)
The length to which people go to satisfy their desire
for wealth is extraordinary. For example, in Sydney,
David Robertson and a partner, Stephen Parylyk,
were reported to have bought an original Picasso
linocut called 'Trois Femmes' for $10,000. They cut
the print into 500 pieces, the size of postage stamps
and were selling them for $190 each, or a total of
$95,000.[9]

The Australian journalist, Philip Adams, says that
he remembers being with Barry Humphries in an

exclusive hattery in Bond Street, London, where Humphries decided to buy the sort of broad-rimmed hat worn by Cecil Beaton. 'This, sir,' said the genuflecting salesman, 'is a bargain.'

'I abhor a bargain,' said Humphries. 'I insist on paying extra.' Adams was right to comment that what was satire for Humphries 'is reassurance for the wealthy. Paying extra is their solace, their religion, their celebration of life.'[10]

In the Christian world, there is a similar, rarely checked enthusiasm for wealth as a celebration of life.

However, Jesus treats the possibility of finding a wealthy disciple as a joke! 'It is easier for a camel to go through the eye of a needle than for someone who is rich to enter the kingdom of God.'[11] This is the kind of humorous impossible situation some would describe as being 'like nailing jelly to the wall' or others, 'trying to find a needle in a haystack'.

The difficulty of wealthy people entering the kingdom of God is said to perplex and to astonish the disciples greatly.[12] This is because they had been raised on a strong Old Testament tradition that wealth was a sign of God's approval of a person. For example, Job, a man said to be the greatest or most wealthy person in the ancient East, is also said to have been blessed and his possessions protected by God.[13] Also, wealth was seen as enabling a person to be charitable in much the same way as wealthy Christians justify their accumulation of wealth by saying that God can use it.[14]

However, Mark has just shown that God's blessing is not related to a person's material possessions. In fact, people can receive from wealth such a false sense of security that it causes them not to follow Jesus.

Those hearing this from Jesus were justly confused, for wealth or material success, one of the key marks of God's approval, had been rejected by Jesus. 'Then who can be saved?' they asked one another (verse 26). This question arose because, in this story, the disciples had been seeing the possibility of salvation from a human perspective. Jesus' reply, 'For mortals it is impossible, but not for God' (verse 27), is to make the point that no human achievement can be successful in gaining a place in God's company. A person's salvation depends entirely on God.

The rewards of obedience
(verses 28 to 31)

Mark's purpose in this paragraph is to generalise and summarise his lessons on wealth and materialism. In Mark, the disciples state not that they had left material possessions or wealth, but that they (as all followers must) had left everything. In fact, the list at the beginning of Jesus' promise ('house or brothers or sister or mother or father or children or fields') was probably intended to cover every aspect of human existence which disciples are required to set aside 'for my sake and for the sake of the good news' (chapter 10, verse 29).

We have seen that, for Mark, the word *euangelion* ('good news') is of strategic importance in what he has to say. The good news is not only about the life and ministry of Jesus; it is also about what the followers of Jesus have to *convey* about Jesus.[15] In short, at the heart of being a follower of Jesus lies the conveying to others of the good news of Jesus.

Mark portrays six characteristics that are rewards for following Jesus:

1. Followers get a new family.
The promise of receiving a hundredfold houses and brothers and sisters and mothers and children and fields, is clearly not meant in the material sense, not least because 'mothers' is plural! Rather, an obedient renunciation of worldy possessions, as well as human relationships, is rewarded by new relationships and a full and satisfied life in the new family of followers of Jesus.

2. The rewards are greater than the losses.
Each item mentioned that is renounced is connected to the next by the word 'or' (verse 29). However, the items in the list of rewards are connected by 'and' (verse 30). The result is the impression that, while individual aspects of life may be renounced to follow Jesus, the rewards are total and much greater.

3. 'Wife' is probably excluded from the renunciation.

It has been noted by others that 'wife' is omitted from these lists.   Could it be that this was one God-given relationship which could not be broken by anything short of martyrdom?[16] We know from Paul that early Christians valued the company of their wives in their missionary travels.[17]

4. The exclusion of 'father' may symbolise
God's place as Father.

While 'father' is listed among what a would-be disciple leaves, there is no mention of a 'father' among the rewards of being a follower of Jesus. Could this be because Mark believed that a fol-lower of Jesus has only one father, the heavenly Father?[18]

5. Persecution is a reward.

This is probably a particularly important idea to Mark. Mark does not explain directly how persecution can be a reward for following Jesus.   However, from his passage about taking up one's cross, he probably understood the privilege of suffering for Jesus' sake to be a complete sharing in the life of Jesus.

6. Followers are in God's company.

The rewards of obedience so far mentioned make it clear that this earthly life of discipleship — including persecution — more than compensates for what has been renounced.

In other words, being a follower of Jesus is not simply waiting for a heavenly reward. Nevertheless, in the age to come — beyond the pain of leaving possessions and relationships and beyond persecution — is the promise of eternal life, or being in God's company.

The final verse, 'many who are first will be last, and the last will be first' (verse 31), makes the point of the lessons on wealth and materialism. Wealth is not in itself an indication of God's blessing. Those who put their trust in it are not followers of Jesus and will not receive eternal life. On the other hand, those who have abandoned everything to follow Jesus will be first — they will receive that life.

This passage has enabled Mark to teach his readers at least three important lessons:

* *Discipleship involves a gracious miracle.* While it is impossible for anyone to achieve anything to bring about salvation or make it possible to be a follower of Jesus, a gracious miracle of God makes it possible.
* *Total renunciation is required of the potential disciple.*
* *Discipleship means both present and future rewards.* Total renunciation is rewarded not only in the future life, but in the present family of followers of Jesus. Even persecution is a reward, for it enables a follower of Jesus with an otherwise impossible opportunity to identify with him.

Discussion questions

Talking it through

1 What does the story of the rich man show about discipleship? What has wealth to do with it?

2 What new idea is Jesus injecting into the debate with his reply in verse 27? How does this make you feel?

3 Do you see Jesus as undermining the family unit in verses 28 to 31?

4 How far do you think this passage indicates that the rewards of discipleship are in this life, and how far does it suggest that they are in the next?

Widening our horizons

1 Do any of the following stand as barriers between you and discipleship:
(a) money?
(b) sex?
(c) power?
   Rank them according to the seriousness of the threat each poses to you. Is there overlap?

2 What do you normally do in the following situation:
(a) when someone asks you for food or money?
(b) when an aid organisation asks for support?
(c) when a family member asks for a loan?
   Are your responses usually in the positive or negative? What affects your decision?

3 Are you holding on to possessions tightly or loosely at the moment? Which things are you holding on to most tightly? Why?

4 Do you think you could be very rich and still have a clear conscience? Why or why not? How much is too much?

8
Glory and suffering

What can we expect of Jesus' disciples?
MARK CHAPTER 10, VERSES 32 TO 45

THE FATE OF JESUS AND HIS FOLLOWERS was by now undeniably and abundantly clear.

The goal of suffering and death
(verses 32 to 34)
For Mark's first readers, the first tightly packed sentence (verse 32) would have been full of pathos. Jesus is depicted as walking ahead of his followers in a way customary for Jewish teachers as they travelled with their followers. But why are the followers of Jesus said to be amazed and afraid?

Jesus and those with him are said to be 'on the road'. From Mark's use of this phrase in conjunction with Jesus' other saying about his tragic future, Mark's readers are being reminded that Jesus' 'way' is the way of suffering and death. Then, although this is the first time Jerusalem is mentioned as the destination of the journey, what Mark's readers already know is clearly portrayed; the goal of Jesus' life and ministry is suffering and death in the city — the fount of hostility to Jesus and the place where many of God's messengers have come to a similar end.[1] In a moment this will be reinforced when, through Jesus' words, Mark repeats that Jesus is 'going up to Jerusalem' (verse 33).

Up until this stage in Mark's story, the Twelve and the other followers had not understood the fate of Jesus. Here, as Jesus is depicted as 'going up to Jerusalem', they were amazed and afraid, for at last they began to understand that Jesus' end was suffering and death.

A careful reading of verse 32 suggests that 'they' (the Twelve) were amazed, while 'those who followed' — other disciples, including women — were afraid.[2] It could be that the Twelve, knowing so much about Jesus, were amazed that God's anointed should have chosen the fate of shame, suffering and death. In that the Twelve represent all followers of Jesus, Mark is probably telling his readers that amazement is the most natural and appropriate response to the Son of God's choosing the fate of suffering and death, especially as it was a death for others.[3]

It could be that the other followers of Jesus were afraid, for they were to lose their leader and may have been expected to suffer the same fate. It could also be that 'those who followed' are intended to represent Mark's readers — those under persecution who fear the same fate as their Master.

However, in the following story in verses 38 to 41 — where members of the Twelve, without reference to shame and suffering, request a significant share in glory — it is clear that they do not yet fully understand or do not want to face the prospect of Jesus' shameful and painful death.

It was to be Bartimaeus who would be the first to follow Jesus most eagerly 'on the way' to Jerusalem and to suffering and death. Yet Mark has signalled to his readers that such an end is also the calling of the followers of Jesus.

Even though they were to fail in the darkest moments, Jesus would not abandon them, but continues to lead them. Mark indicates this through the word 'go before' (*proagō*) in verse 32. On the Mount of Olives, as the shadow of the cross fell more darkly over the story, Jesus would say to his followers: 'You will all become deserters' (chapter 14, verse 28). But Jesus still undertook to lead (*proagō*) them.

Despite protestation from Peter, they all scattered, not willing to share in any of Jesus' shame, suffering and death. Yet, true to his word, at the very end of this Gospel, Jesus is reported as saying that he would 'go before' (*proagō*) or lead his followers into Galilee, the place symbolic of Jesus' presence and powerful ministry amongst the crowds and his followers.[4]

For a third time (verses 33 to 34), Jesus predicted his shameful suffering and death. So detailed is this prophecy that many students of Mark suggest that it was formulated after the event. Jesus, however, would have been well aware of the impact his ministry would have had on the religious and political authorities. He would also have been well aware of the fate of so many other prophets of the past. Also, Mark has not tried to conform the wording of this passage to what he says about its fulfilment in chapter 15, verse 15. Indeed, the order of events in verse 34 is the reverse order in chapter 15, verses 15 to 20.

Verse 33 begins with the word 'See'. Compared with Matthew and Luke, Mark and John use 'see' or 'listen' (*idou*) infrequently and to demand special attention of the reader.[5] Here Mark is probably drawing attention to two things. First, Mark is drawing attention to Jerusalem being the destination of the journey. Second, he wanted the readers to note that it was not only Jesus who was going to Jerusalem, but his followers as well. Once again, Mark emphasises that being a follower of Jesus involves following a way of shame and suffering.

The difficulty followers find in carrying out this call was to be illustrated by Mark in the tragic story of Peter's denial in chapter 14, verses 66 to 72. Mercifully, as we have just noted, Mark also portrays Jesus' gracious forgiveness of his followers' failures by saying that Jesus would continue to lead his disciples as their companion and teacher as they come from/go to the place of learning from Jesus.[6]

In verse 33, the phrase 'will be handed over' could be a reference to Judas 'betraying' or 'handing over' Jesus, for it was the same word that was used for Judas in chapter 14, verse 44. However, the passive tense of the verb (*paradothēsetai* here) is often used respectfully to avoid a direct mention of God.[7] Thus, once again, Mark is probably drawing attention to the death of Jesus being under the control of God.[8]

One of the most significant differences between this and the two earlier predictions of Jesus' suffering and death was the mention of the Jewish authorities handing Jesus over to the Gentiles.

For Mark, the Gentiles are foreigners or outsiders — those who are ignorant of the good news. They are also those for whom God cares and whom he wants to hear the good news.[9] For Jesus to be handed over by the Jews to the Gentiles was to be betrayed by God's own people. This image is a figure of the rejection of the followers of Jesus into the hands of those who have yet to understand the good news of Jesus. In verse 34, there is a hint of what will soon be made explicit in verse 45: the suffering of Jesus is not in vain, but is on behalf of others. Mark's readers would have gathered this from the Old Testament passages echoed here.

In Isaiah, a servant is depicted as suffering by being mocked or ridiculed, spat upon and killed, just as Jesus was.[10] Mark's readers would have known that Isaiah also says that his servant 'was wounded for our transgressions, crushed for our iniquities; upon him was the punishment that made us whole. . .' (chapter 53, verse 5). Mark's readers would also probably have identified Jesus with Isaiah — the servant's life was an offering for sin and was to put many people in a right relationship with God.[11]

A request for glory (verses 35 to 37)

Each time Mark records Jesus predicting his dreadful end, he shows the disciples' misunderstanding of him. Mark now portrays the disciples as only hearing part of what Jesus said. They heard that Jesus was going up to Jerusalem, but not that he was going there to suffer. One of the reasons messianic pretenders went up to Jerusalem was to establish their sovereignty or kingship.

As Mark tells the story, the disciples had heard only of the impending glory to be attained by Jesus. In turn, James and John — perhaps representing those who do not understand God's way to glory — quickly seized an opportunity to be part of the glory they anticipated to be Jesus'.

The request (in verse 37) to sit on either side of Jesus in his glory could have meant sitting in the places of honour at the celebratory feast at the end of time. However, from the other two occasions Mark uses 'glory' (*doxa*, in chapter 8, verse 38 and chapter 13, verse 26), the word signifies Jesus' obvious regency for God at the end of time. Thus, James and John were asking to sit in the places of highest honour as Jesus rules the world for his Father. The selfish and cheap understanding of this request will become apparent as the passage unfolds.

A response of suffering (verses 38 to 40)

Verses 38 and 39 show that the disciples did not realise what they were asking, for they did not realise that glory did not come without suffering.

The image of 'the cup' in verse 38 carries a double meaning. On the one hand, to share someone's drink was to share the same fate. For example, as Polycarp, the Bishop of Smyrna (on the west coast of modern Turkey) was being prepared to be burnt at the stake in about AD 155, he prayed thankfully that he was able to share the cup of Christ.[12]

On the other hand, the cup was also an Old Testament image for the anger of God against human

wrong and rebellion.[13]   Therefore, for Mark to say
that Jesus was about to drink the cup of God's anger
against sin, he would probably have been conveying
the idea that Jesus was standing in for the punishment of the sin of others.   This view will be
confirmed in a moment in verse 45.

So, Jesus' question 'Are you able to die the death
I will die?' must receive 'No' for an answer. Their
suffering and possible martyrdom would not save
others. Yet the disciples' suffering and the suffering
of all Christians in following Jesus could be a means
whereby others hear the good news of Jesus.

The baptism referred to in verse 39 is Jesus' death.
In the Old Testament, to be drowned in water was
a metaphor for undergoing the most terrible
tragedy.[14] For Jews in Mark's time and later, to be
drowned was to die the most cruel kind of death.[15]
Not surprisingly, Paul uses the idea of baptism to
illustrate the idea of dying with Christ.[16]

James and John are shown as naively confident
that they could 'drink the cup' and 'be baptised' as
Jesus would be. Still the disciples, represented by
these two, did not seem to comprehend the profound
cost of following Jesus. Jesus then affirmed that they
would indeed suffer the same fate. The readers of
Mark may have known that Herod killed James with
a sword[17] and that John, while not being martyred,
was exiled on the Island of Patmos, fifty-five
kilometres off the south-west coast of Asia Minor.[18]

So far in Jesus' words, the emphasis had always been on the suffering involved in being a follower of his. Thought of reward or glory, relegated to the background, comes to the fore in verses 35 to 40. Perhaps because of the frailty of human nature and temptation to eschew suffering and seek easy alternatives, Mark says Jesus focussed attention on the necessity and inevitability of suffering. The reward was neither his concern, nor his to give.

It is a principle well-known in the New Testament that any present or future reward or glory in being a Christian is preceded by suffering. Thus, Paul wrote to the Philippians that he wanted to share Christ's 'suffering by becoming like him in death, if somehow I may attain the resurrection from the dead' (chapter 3, verses 10 and 11). And the writer of 1 Peter encouraged his readers to 'rejoice in so far as you are sharing Christ's sufferings so that you may also be glad and shout for joy when his glory is revealed' (chapter 4, verse 13).

However, no New Testament writer, and certainly not Mark, saw the glory and joy following any suffering as a just reward. Glory is a gift! In just three words ('but those prepared') the Greek implies that God will give the gift of glory to those of his choice.

Leadership and internal relationships (verses 41 to 44)

James and John misunderstood the nature of

discipleship. Here is a second story showing the
disciples misunderstanding the fate of Jesus and its
implications for his followers. It is a variation on
the theme of the first story. In this story, Mark gives
teaching on the behaviour appropriate for Christian
leadership. From the context — the sayings on the
death of Jesus in verses 33 and 34, and the ransom
saying in verse 45 — what Jesus said about the
nature of leadership was based on its expression of
greatness in his own life.

❏ *Pagan leadership (verse 42)*
Mark contrasts pagan and Christian leadership. In
the Greek, the Gentile or pagan leaders are ironically
described as 'so-called rulers' (verse 42). The irony
is that, while they are called leaders, they are in
reality tyrants exploiting their people. For example,
Antiochus IV, who ruled over Syria including Palestine
from 175 to 164 BC, struck coins carrying the inscription
'King Antiochus, God Manifest'.[19] Yet he is reported
to have slaughtered tens of thousands of Jews in a
few days and pillaged the Temple in Jerusalem.[20]

❏ *Christian leadership (verses 43 and 44)*
Christian leadership is described in sharp contrast
to this. A Christian leader, or one who wishes to
be 'great', must be a servant (*diakonos*) of those being
led (verse 43). To put it another way, whoever
wishes to be first, or lead, must be a slave (*doulos*)
of all (verse 44).

'Servant' or 'slave' may be synonymous, or Mark may be shedding light on two important aspects of Christian leadership.

'Servant' (*diakonos*) can be taken to refer to the *activity* of the Christian leaders. A servant's activities are not self-interested, but are directed to the good of another. One of the most common activities of a servant was the menial task of waiting on tables. We would conclude from this that Christian leadership ought not to be for the benefit of the leaders, but for those who are following. This perspective was modelled well by Paul. He saw his ministry of evangelism in being a slave of those he sought to win.[21]

'Slave' (*doulos*) can be taken to refer to the *status* of the Christian leader. A slave had no life of his own; he belonged to another. We can conclude from this that a Christian leader's life belongs to the group of disciples being led. However, we cannot conclude from what Mark says that the leader is the slave to every demand and criticism of the community. At the risk of putting too much weight on a single word, it is worth noting that Mark does not say that the leader is the slave of *each* (*hekastos*) person but of *all* (*pas*) or the whole group.

His life a ransom for many (verse 45)

This verse is one of the most famous sentences in the whole of Mark and it is the model, means and summary for all that has just been said in this section about relationships among the followers of Jesus. Almost every word is significant for what Mark is saying.

The term 'Son of Man' for Mark is the title which best sums up the identity of Jesus. In this title, Mark can hold in tension three elements: Jesus the glorious chosen Son of God, who has power over Satan, storms and sin; Jesus, the one who serves by suffering for others; and Jesus who will come again one day, in the obvious and marvellous power of God, to be judge.

Mark is putting in a nutshell the nature of Jesus' ministry. The word 'he comes', *elthen*, sums up for him the entire ministry of Jesus.[22] Also, Mark's readers would have seen it as a veiled allusion to Jesus coming from God.

The term 'to serve' in verse 45 is the model on which Mark built his teaching of relationships in the Christian community. Mark makes this plain by using 'for' (*gar*), to tie this saying about Jesus to what has just been said. The disinterested care Jesus' followers are to show towards each other, and which is to characterise Christian leadership, is now seen to be exemplified in Jesus.

In the final section of Mark (from chapter 11, verse 1), Mark's readers will have before them the shame, suffering and the great act of selfless care by Jesus: his undeserved death.

In the phrase 'to give his life', readers of Mark would have found poignant echoes of others who had voluntarily given their lives. Jews equated the phrase with martyrs and Greeks equated it with soldiers giving their lives.[23] The context here indicates that Mark is not only telling us about the nature of Jesus' ministry. He is also telling us about the profound service Christians are to offer each other!

The word 'ransom' (*lutron*) is only used here and in the parallel passage in Matthew 20, verse 28 in the New Testament. In the ancient world, as in our own, a ransom was paid for the recovery of a hostage or to free a slave.[24] In the light of the whole sentence, the Greek word *anti* ('for') means 'instead of' or 'in place of' rather than 'on behalf of'. That is, Jesus is dying in our place, says Mark.

At face value, 'many' (*polus*) could lead us to think that Jesus gave his life for a limited number of people. However, in both Aramaic and Greek, 'many' can mean 'all'.[25] Not surprisingly, then, a very similar sentence in 1 Timothy 2, verse 6 reads, 'he gave himself a ransom (*antilutron*) for all (*pas*).'[26]

In Mark's use of 'servant' and the phrase 'for many' in this passage, he probably intended us to have in mind Isaiah 53, about a servant suffering for the sins of others. Yet, as some Jews used 'many' to refer to God's people,[27] the idea is also present that, while Jesus gave his life for everyone, not everyone will choose to experience the benefits of his death.

Discussion questions

Talking it through

1 Mark's original readers probably suffered persecution. What comfort was there in verses 32 to 34 for them? What comfort is there in them for us?

2 In what way can Jesus' followers follow him (verses 39 to 40)? Is this the sort of discipleship James and John had in mind in verse 37?

3 What, in your view, are the reasons that Christians place such importance on verse 45?

4 What are the radical features of discipleship that are mentioned in verses 35 to 45? What is so different about them?

Widening our horizons

1 Rejection is difficult to face. We see how Jesus handled the prospect of rejection in these verses. What is the worst rejection you have faced? How did you handle it? Could you have done better?

2 Is there anything or anyone you are willing to die for? If you would, why would you be willing to pay that price — or why not?

3 Jesus' communication difficulty in teaching the nature of discipleship to the disciples in Mark is a problem we have all faced. One helpful technique in the difficult process of ideas being transferred from one mind to another is for the hearer to say: 'What I hear you as saying is. . .'

What other techniques can you think of that help in this process? Why is there often such a difficulty in us truly understanding what another says?

4 While we do not generally have leaders who 'lord it over us' like Antiochus IV did, how can each of the following show this characteristic in some measure:

(a) a head of government (president, prime minister, premier, etc.)?
(b) an employer?
(c) a spouse?
(d) a parent?

9
A model for disciples

What is the right way to follow Jesus?
MARK CHAPTER 10, VERSES 46 TO 52

They threw down their nets
and they followed him.
There was no time to
calculate profit or loss.
There was no time to
call home for a second opinion.
It seemed like absolute madness.
It seemed like death.
The old faith dropped
and sank beneath waves.
The new faith walked on water,
beckoned on to Jerusalem
and the dry hills around.[1]

THE SECTION OF MARK with which we are dealing in this book began in chapter 8, verses 22 to 26 with a story of a man who was at first only partially healed of blindness. We have since seen that the disciples only partially understood the teaching mission and destiny of Jesus and its implications for them. This section of Mark on discipleship ends, sadly, without the disciples receiving full insight. Indeed, right to the end of the Gospel, the disciples never fully understand Jesus and the implications of following him.

Yet the Gospel ends portraying Jesus as willing to forgive profound failure and lead his followers. Mark implies that it is the resurrection which will open the eyes of the disciples and allow them to follow Jesus as enthusiastically as Bartimaeus.

In the last story in this section on discipleship, Mark depicts an outsider comprehending that, having received sight from Jesus, the appropriate response is to follow him on his fateful journey to Jerusalem. That an outsider should comprehend the nature of discipleship may be Mark's way of emphasising the simplicity of being a follower of Jesus.

A critical stage in the journey (verse 46)

Mark's Gospel began with John the Baptist preparing the way for Jesus. Then Jesus called disciples to follow him. He leads, feeds and instructs his followers along the way — a way that has a fateful destiny in Jerusalem. The story of Bartimaeus marks a critical point in this journey. Its importance is heightened by its being the last healing story in Mark.

Three times in this single sentence, Mark draws attention to Jesus, his disciples and a large crowd being on a journey: they came to Jericho, they left Jericho, and Bartimaeus was sitting by the roadside.

Jesus' teaching on discipleship is completed and Jericho is the last town along the way before they reach the outskirts of Jerusalem. This is a last graphic demonstration of what it means to be a follower of Jesus. Not only does Mark have the disciples observe the miracle; there is a large crowd of followers — perhaps representing the great mass of later Christians — who also need to know what it means to be a follower of Jesus.

Bartimaeus is portrayed as blind. Many who heard this story would have been able to identify with Bartimaeus. Plant poison, snake and insect bites, accidents, war wounds, illness and blinding as a punishment made blindness common. Blindness was also thought of as a punishment for sin and excluded a Jew from being a priest.[2]

The blind were used as slaves in mines and in breaking stones. Some blind people tried to scratch out an existence through singing or making music. But, because most professions were closed to the blind, they lived in extreme poverty and were the epitome of helplessness, need and weakness, requiring legal protection.[3] Mark heightens the need of the character in his story by saying that Bartimaeus was a beggar.

It is likely that there were operations for cataracts by the third century BC. But it was thought that the cure of blindness required a miracle.[4]

However, Mark would not have chosen to record a story about curing a blind person simply because it was a difficult or miraculous healing. Its metaphorical meaning would have been just as important to Mark. Thus, those who were morally and intellectually defective were said to be blind. Those who did not know God's salvation were said to be wandering around blindly. Importantly for Mark's theme of the disciples' lack of understanding, blindness was a metaphor frequently used for a lack of knowledge and understanding, especially about the future.

Considering again Mark's story of the so-called rich young ruler in chapter 10, verses 17 to 22, it is interesting to note that, in the ancient world, wealth was thought to be the primary cause of intellectual and moral blindness. So Bartimaeus being blind would have enabled Mark to use the story to represent the lack of understanding of the disciples.

Only twice, here and in the story of Jairus' daughter (chapter 5, verse 22), does Mark use a name for a character. Such a reminiscence certainly makes the story personal.

Because of the significance of 'way' or 'road' in Mark's story, it is pertinent that Bartimaeus was sitting alongside the road. Mark probably wanted his readers to note that he was not yet a follower of Jesus — he was not yet travelling along the road.

Jesus save me! (verses 47 to 49)

Bartimaeus, the helpless beggar, is seen as recognising that Jesus could help him. By calling Jesus the 'Son of David', he sees him as a healer who brings salvation. The name 'Son of David' would have called to mind Solomon who, at the time Mark was writing, had a great reputation as a healer.[5] While 'Son of David' is not a dominant title for Jesus in Mark, it is clearly an aspect of Jesus' ministry Mark wanted to affirm, because Jesus did not contradict or correct Bartimaeus.

Mark's readers would have seen that the cry of Bartimaeus was not simply for healing. A cry for 'mercy' from Bartimaeus was a cry for God's anointed messenger to show love by removing God's wrath from his life and to bring salvation.[6] Later Christians commonly used receiving sight as a way of talking about receiving salvation.[7]

Jesus heeded the plea for salvation and directed those around to bring the blind man to him.

❏ *Leaving the past behind (verses 50 to 52)*
The dramatic action of throwing off one's cloak, as

Bartimaeus did in verse 50, was a powerful symbol of throwing off the past. In Colossians 3, verses 9 and 10, Paul used the idea of putting off an old piece of clothing and putting on a new piece as a way of representing leaving the old life to take up the new life of a Christian.[8] Mark's readers would have known that for a person to be said to put on the cloak of a philosopher was to say that the person had become a follower of the philosopher.[9]

Bartimaeus was healed or, as the story emphasises, received salvation because of his faith (*pistis*). Now that 'faith' has come to mean 'something *a person* has or generates to help believe something', it ought to be exchanged for the word 'trust'. Trust better translates the biblical word *pistis* with its idea of confidence or trust which God engenders in a person.

When we look back through the story, we see a number of points where Mark has drawn attention to Bartimaeus' words and actions as evidence of his trust:

* Despite many sternly ordering him to stop calling to Jesus, he kept calling for mercy or salvation (verse 48).
* When Jesus stopped to call him, Bartimaeus was told to 'take heart' (*tharsei*) — that is, be confident or trusting (verse 49).
* When he was called, the blind beggar sprang or leapt up in response (verse 50).

∗ When Bartimaeus was asked what he wanted, his request was like a prayer, using the reverent word 'Rabbouni', or 'My Lord, let me see' (verse 51).[10]

Immediately Jesus said he was well, he was! The response to being healed — saved — sums up much that Mark has been saying about discipleship. The proper response to being called by Jesus — to receiving God's mercy from him — is, like Bartimaeus, to follow Jesus voluntarily on the way of discipleship. This was to be possible after the resurrection when the disciples were to experience the presence of the risen Lord and receive the Holy Spirit.[11]

Discussion questions

Talking it through

1 In Mark, there are two groups of disciples: the official ones, and the unofficial ones like Bartimaeus, a number of women and other marginalised people. Why does the second group generally get discipleship right?

2 What does Bartimaeus' appeal for 'mercy' show us about his understanding of the link between suffering and sin? Do you believe the two are linked? How?

3 Why does Jesus heal Bartimaeus? If everyone isn't healed, is the reason for this given in verse 52?

4 What does Mark suggest is the hallmark of a disciple?

Widening our horizons

1 Try saying the story of Bartimaeus dramatically. If possible, learn it off by heart and say it dramatically to a friend. It can easily be learnt by breaking it into sections — first, the setting (verse 46); second, Bartimaeus' first call (verse 47); third, Bartimaeus' second call, (verse 48); fourth, Jesus' response (verse 49); fifth, Bartimaeus' action (verse 50); sixth, dialogue (verse 51), seventh, Jesus' healing (verse 52).

How do you think written stories like this might have originated? Does the story have more power when said like this? Can you think of situations where such dramatic reading can be helpful?

2 Why is it inappropriate that we should seek to engender in others the same trust of us as Jesus sought to engender in himself? In your answer, consider the following areas, situations of trust:

(a) the trust sexually abusive parents seek to engender

    (b) the trust political dictators seek to engender

    (c) the trust a manipulative sales person seeks to engender.

3 How can each of the following model being a disciple in their dealings with those under their authority:

(a) an employer?

(b) a parent?

(c) a church leader?

    What changes in the organisation might need to be made in each case?

4 Is discipleship worth it? Is the call of Jesus to suffering and persecution, even for his sake, just too hard to bear? Compare this passage in Mark with Matthew 5, verse 10.

    Does all suffering have an immediate point to it? What do you say to someone experiencing inexplicable suffering?

Endnotes

Foreword
1. Saint Augustine, *The Trinity*, 15: 28

Introduction
1. Acts 12: 12, 25; 13: 13; 15: 37–39; Colossians 4: 10; 2 Timothy 4: 11; Philemon 24; 1 Peter 5: 13
2. Mark 14: 51–52
3. Irenaeus, *Against Heretics*, 3.1.1
4. Mark 13: 2, 14; Luke 21: 20–24
5. Tacitus, *Histories*, 2.8.2
6. Mark 13: 14
7. Mark 2: 18–3: 6; 7: 1-23; 10: 35–45
8. Mark 9: 14–29; 9: 33–50; 10: 10–12; 11: 20–26
9. Mark 1: 17; 3: 14; 6: 7–13
10. Mark 3: 31–35
11. Mark 1: 9, 24; 10: 47; 14: 67; 16: 6
12. Mark 3: 21, 31–35; 11: 12–19; 14: 32–42; 15: 34–37
13. Mark 1: 1, 34; 8: 29; 9: 41; 12: 35; 13: 21; 14: 61; 15: 32
14. Mark 14: 62
15. Mark 1: 11; 3: 11; 5: 7; 9: 7; (14: 61); 15: 39 and, in some manuscripts, 1: 1. The words 'Son of God' are not found in

some very important manuscripts (for example, the fourth century codex Sinaiticus, the ninth century codex Koridethi and an eleventh century manuscript in the Bibliotheque Nationale in Paris (known as 28). On the other hand, the fourth century codex Vaticaus, the fifth or sixth century codex Bezae and the twelfth century Washington codex, among others, including early Church fathers, give good support for Mark writing the phrase 'Son of God'. Thus, in modern New Testament Greek texts, the phrase is printed in brackets.

16. See M. Hengel, *The Son of God*, SCM, 1976

17. Mark 4: 9–13

18. Mark 3: 11; 8: 27–9: 1; 15: 39

19. See, e.g., Mark 2: 27–28; 8: 31; 9: 9–12, 31; 10: 45

20. Mark 2: 10; 8: 38; 13: 26; 14: 62

21. Mark 4: 13

22. Mark 6: 51–52; 8: 33; 10: 13–16, 23–27

23. Mark 9: 18–19

24. Mark 14: 50

25. T.J. Weedon, *Mark — Traditions in Conflict*, Fortress, 1971, pp.50–51

26. Mark 6: 30; 14: 72; 16: 7

27. E. Best, *Disciples and Discipleship*, T.&T. Clark, 1980, pp.119–121

28. Mark 9: 28–29; 10: 10–11

29. E. Best, *Following Jesus: Discipleship in the Gospel of Mark*, JSOT, 1981, pp.9-14; Elizabeth Malbon, 'Disciples/Crowds/Whoever: Markan Characters and Readers', *Novum Testamentum*, 28, 1986, pp.104–130

30. Mark 1: 16–20; 10: 23–31

31. Mark 3: 14; 15: 18

32. Mark 6: 13; 9: 14–29

33. Mark 8: 31–38

34. Mark 9: 18–19, 28–29, 33–37; 14: 66–72. See also 10: 35–45.

35. Mark 14: 72; 16: 7
36. The ancient sources for this information are given by G. Friedrich, *Theological Dictionary of the New Testament*, Vol.2, Eerdmans, 1964, pp.722–725.
37. Mark 1: 14–15
38. Mark 1: 11
39. See Mark 1: 4–14; 6: 14–29.
40. Mark 8: 11–21
41. Mark 8: 27; 9: 33–34; 10: 32, 52
42. Mark 8: 27; 9: 33–34
43. Mark 10: 46–52
44. Mark 10: 32–34
45. Mark 8: 31–33; 9: 30–32; 10: 32–34
46. Mark 1: 10–11
47. Mark 9: 28–29
48. Best, *Disciples and Discipleship*, pp.15–16

Chapter 1

1. Mark 8: 14–21
2. Mark 6: 35–44; 8: 1–10
3. Mark 8: 18, 21
4. Mark 8: 22–26 and 10: 46–52
5. Mark 7: 24, 31; 8: 10, 13, 22, 27
6. Mark 6: 45
7. Matthew 11: 21; Luke 10: 13
8. *Babylonian Talmud Nedarim*, 64b
9. See, e.g., Isaiah 29: 18; 35: 5; 42: 6.
10. See, e.g., Josephus, *Jewish Antiquities*, 6.25.
11. Mark 1: 40; 6: 56; 7: 32
12. Mark 5: 35–43
13. Suetonius, *The Twelve Caesars: Vespasian*, 7
14. *The Genesis Apocryphon*, 20
15. H. van der Loos, *The Miracles of Jesus*, Brill, 1965, pp.313–321

16. Mark 5: 24b–34
17. Mark 5: 1–20
18. Mark 8: 27–30
19. For example, see also Mark 1: 44–45; 5: 53; 7: 36; 8: 26.
20. *The Messianic Secret*, SPCK and Fortress
21. Mark 1: 45; 5: 19–20; 7: 36–37
22. Mark 1: 11
23. Mark 8: 29; 10: 47–48
24. Josephus, *Jewish Antiquities*, 18: 26–28
25. Josephus, *Jewish Antiquities*, 15.363
26. See, E. Schurer, *The History of the Jewish People in the Age of Jesus Christ*, Vol.2, T.&T. Clark, 1979, pp.169–171.
27. Mark 1: 3; Isaiah 40: 1–11
28. Mark 9: 12
29. See 2 Kings 1: 8 and Mark 1: 6
30. Mark 1: 4–5
31. Mark 1: 2–3; 1: 4; 14–15; 2: 18; 6: 29 and 1: 16–20; 3: 13–19; 1: 5 and 3: 7–9; 1: 7–8 and 8: 31; 9: 31; 10: 33–34; 11: 31 and 12: 1–12; 14: 63–64; 6: 14–29 and 15: 1–5
32. Mark 1: 7–8
33. Mark 6: 15. Elijah is mentioned in Mark at 6: 15; 8: 28; 9: 4, 5, 11–13; 15: 35–36
34. Mark 9: 11–13
35. O. Cullmann, *The Christology of the New Testament*, SCM, 1963
36. Mark 6: 15
37. Mark 4: 11–12
38. Mark 6: 14–16
39. Psalm 18; 78: 65–72; Amos 9: 11–12; Isaiah 9: 11; Zechariah 4: 6–10; Psalms of Solomon 17: 5–8, 23–28, 32; *Manual of Discipline*, 9: 11. See also R.A. Horsley with J.S. Hanson, *Bandits, Prophets and Messiahs*, Harper and Row, 1988, Ch.3.
40. 1 Samuel 10: 1, 6; 16: 13; Isaiah 61: 1
41. Mark 1: 1
42. Mark 1: 34

43.   Mark 8: 30

Chapter 2

1.   J. Calvin, *Institutes of the Christian Religion*, 3.8.1
2.   For more on the title 'Son of Man' in Mark, see I.H. Marshall, in J.B. Green et al., *Dictionary of Jesus and the Gospels*, IVP, 1992, pp.775–781
3.   Mark 8: 9–30
4.   Mark 8: 31
5.   Mark 9: 7, 9
6.   See, for example, Ignatius, *Ephesians*, 20: 2; *Barnabas*, 12: 10; Irenaeus, *Against Heretics*, 3.16.7; Justin, *Dialogues*, 76.1; 100; *Odes of Solomon* 36: 3.
7.   See also, Mark 13: 26; 14: 62.
8.   Mark 8: 31, 38; 9: 9, 12, 31; 10: 33, 45; 14: 21, 41. Other references to the Son of Man in Mark are 2: 10, 28; 13: 26; 14: 62.
9.   Mark 10: 45
10.   Mark 13: 26–27
11.   Mark 9: 12; compare 14: 21, 49.
12.   Many translations, including the NRSV, do not make this clear.
13.   Mark 2: 2; 4: 33; 5: 36; 8: 32; 14: 39. See also, for example, Acts 4: 29, 31; 8: 25; 11: 19; 13: 46; 14: 25; 16: 6; 20: 38.
14.   Mark 8: 34
15.   Mark 4: 33–34; 6: 14-15; 8: 27–28
16.   For example, Mark 1: 27; 2: 12; 6: 2
17.   Mark 8: 34
18.   Mark 1: 16–20; 2: 14; 10: 21
19.   Mark 14: 68
20.   All we know of Telemachus is a paragraph in Theodoret's *History of the Church*, 5.26. For the legendary details, see

W. Barclay, *The Gospel of Mark*, Saint Andrew Press, 1954, pp.208–210.

21. Dietrich Bonhoeffer, *The Cost of Discipleship*, SCM, 1959, p.57
22. Josephus, *The Life*, 420
23. Galatians 2: 20
24. Luke 9: 23
25. Mark 13: 10; 14: 9
26. Mark 1: 1–15
27. Mark 10: 17–22
28. See Matthew 5: 21ff; 11: 11; Luke 11: 20; 17: 20–21.
29. Mark 1: 1–15
30. Mark 9: 2–13
31. M. Hengel, *The Charismatic Leader and His Followers*, T. & T. Clark, 1981, pp.86–88

Chapter 3

1. Mark 9: 2
2. Mark 1: 11, 24, 34; 3: 11; 5: 7. See also Morna D. Hooker, 'What Doesn't Thou Here, Elijah?' A Look at St Mark's Account of the Transfiguration', in *The Glory of Christ in the New Testament*, L.D. Hurst and N.T. Wright (eds), Clarendon, 1987, pp.59–70.
3. Exodus 24: 15–18
4. Exodus 24: 12–18; 1 Kings 18: 20; 19: 8, 11; Matthew 5: 1; 28: 16
5. See Mark 2: 25; 3: 26; 4: 2, 5; 5: 15; 7: 15, 21, 33; 9: 2; 14: 1, 43, 61; 15: 26.
6. Mark 9: 3
7. 1 Esdras 8: 57; Nahum 3: 3
8. See Origen, *Against Celsus*, 3.55; W. Lane, *The Gospel of Mark*, Marshall, Morgan and Scott, 1974, p.315 n.9.
9. Daniel 12: 3; 2 Baruch 51: 3, 5, 10, 12; 1 Enoch 38: 4; 104: 2; 4 Ezra 7: 97

10. See Luke 1: 11; 22: 43; 25: 34; Acts 2: 3; 7: 2, 26; 9: 17; 13: 31; 16: 9; 26: 16; 1 Corinthians 15: 5–8.
11. Mark 9: 5
12. Leviticus 23: 40–43
13. Mark 4: 41
14. Mark 5: 36
15. Mark 6: 50
16. Mark 9: 32
17. Mark 8: 27–30
18. Exodus 24: 15-18
19. Mark 13: 26; 14: 62
20. Mark 9: 1
21. Mark 1: 11; 9: 7
22. Mark 1: 24; 3: 11; 5: 7
23. See note 1 of chapter 1.
24. Mark 14: 61
25. Mark 15: 39
26. Mark 1: 11; 9: 7
27. Mark 12: 1–12
28. Mark 1: 24; compare Psalm 106: 16; 2 Kings 4: 9.
29. Genesis 3: 17; 42: 21–22; Exodus 19: 5-8; Judges 2: 17
30. Mark 4: 33
31. Mark 9: 4, 23; compare 8: 18.
32. Mark 4: 10–12; 7: 14
33. John Calvin, commentary on Mark 9: 7; T.H. Parker, *Calvin's New Testament Commentaries*, Eerdmans, 1978, Vol.2, p.201
34. Mark 9: 10
35. Compare Mark 8: 38.
36. Mark 6: 14, 16; 12: 18–27
37. See also Sirach 48: 10; Ezra 6: 26.
38. Compare 1 Kings 19: 1–10 and Mark 6: 14–29.

Chapter 4

1. Mark 3: 19b–30
2. Mark 3: 31–35
3. Mark 4: 1–34
4. Mark 4: 35–41; 5: 1–43
5. Mark 6: 2
6. Mark 6: 7–13
7. Mark 1: 21–28
8. Mark 3: 28–30; see also 3: 15; 6: 7
9. Mark 9: 15
10. *Ekthambeomai,* Mark 9: 15; 14: 33; 16: 5 and *thambeomai,* Mark 1: 27; 10: 24,32
11. Exodus 34: 29–30
12. Mark 1: 21–28
13. See, e.g., *Demon Possession,* J.W. Montgomery (ed.), Bethany House, 1976.
14. Mark 9: 18
15. Mark 2: 17; 5: 4; 9: 18; 14: 37. See also *ischuros,* the noun in Mark 1: 7; 3: 27.
16. Mark 3: 28–30
17. Mark 1: 23; 3: 11; 5: 6–7
18. Mark 9: 18
19. Mark 1: 15; 5: 36; 17: 23–24,31
20. Quoted in C.E.B. Cranfield, *The Gospel According to Saint Mark,* Cambridge University Press, 1966, p.303
21. Mark 9: 24
22. Compare Mark 7: 33; 8: 23
23. Further, see G.H. Twelftree, *Jesus the Exorcist,* J.C.B. Mohr, 1993, chapter 3
24. Mark 3: 22–30
25. Further, see G.H. Twelftree, '*Ekballo ta daimonia,*' in *Gospel Perspectives,* Wenham and C. Blomberg (eds), Vol.6, pp.361–400.
26. Mark 3: 10; 5: 21–43

27. Mark 4: 34; 6: 31–32; 7: 33; 9: 2, 28; 13: 3; 4: 10; 7: 17, 24; 8: 10
28. Mark 4: 34
29. Mark 9: 29
30. G.H. Twelftree, *Christ Triumphant,* Hodder and Stoughton, 1985, pp.40, 121–122

Chapter 5

1. Mark 9: 30
2. Mark 9: 31
3. Mark 4: 29
4. Mark 7: 13; 1 Corinthians 10: 23
5. Mark 1: 14; 15: 15
6. Mark 3: 19; 13: 9–12
7. Mark 3: 19; 14: 10, 11, 18, 21, 41, 42, 44
8. Romans 4: 25; 8: 32
9. See Jeremiah 26: 24.
10. Mark 1: 29
11. Eusebius, *Church History,* 3.39.15
12. Mark 9: 33
13. M. Aberach, 'The Relations Between Master and Disciple in the Talmudic Age', in *Essays Presented to Chief Rabbi Israel Brodie on the Occasion of His Seventieth Birthday,* Soncino Press, 1965
14. Bonhoeffer, *Life Together,* SCM, 1954, p.80
15. Bonhoeffer, *op.cit.,* p.81
16. See, e.g., Ezekiel 8: 1; Matthew 5: 1; Mishnah Aboth 1: 4; 3: 6.
17. Mark 9: 33–34
18. Mark 10: 31, 43–44
19. Compare Josephus, *Jewish Antiquities,* 7.230; 11.141; 19.47; 20.180; Mark 6: 21; Acts 13: 50; 25: 2; 28: 7, 17.
20. Mark 10: 43–45
21. Josephus, *Jewish Antiquities,* 18.21
22. See, e.g. 'The Mekilta,' quoted by C.G. Montefiore and H. Loewe,

      A Rabbinic Anthology, Schocken books, 1974, p.74.

23.   Luke 7: 44
24.   J. Jeremias, *Jerusalem in the Time of Jesus*, SCM, 1969, pp.131–134
25.   As in the Greek tragedies. See, e.g., Aeschylus, *Agamemnon*, 176–178, 249–250.
26.   Bonhoeffer, *Life Together*, SCM, 1954, pp.83–84
27.   Mark 6: 11
28.   Compare Philo of Alexandria, *On the Creation*, 105
29.   Genesis 22: 5; Judges 7: 10; Ruth 2: 5–6; Nehemiah 13: 19
30.   E. Best, *Following Jesus*, JSOT, 1981, p.93, n.32
31.   Mark 6: 11; Luke 16: 4, 9
32.   Compare Luke 2: 28.
33.   Acts 19: 13–16
34.   Mark 9: 33–37
35.   See, e.g., Matthew 6: 1–4.
36.   See, e.g., Matthew 20: 1–16; Luke 17: 7–10.
37.   Despite the paragraphing of the NRSV, it is probably better to take this verse as referring to what goes before rather than what follows, not least because of the mention of 'these' little ones.
38.   Suetonius, *De Vita Caesarum*, 1: 67; Josephus, *Jewish Antiquities*, 14.15.10

Chapter 6

1.   Compare Judith 5: 1; 1 Maccabees 5: 4
2.   See, for example, Romans 16: 17; Wisdom 14: 11.
3.   See Mark 4: 17; 14: 27, 29 and Matthew 18: 7; Romans 16: 17; Revelation 2: 14; Barnabas 4: 9.
4.   Mark 9: 43, 45
5.   Mark 1: 15; 3: 24; 4: 11, 26, 30; 6: 23; 9: 1, 47; 10: 14–15, 23–24, 25; 11: 10; 12: 34; 13: 8; 14: 25; 15: 43
6.   Probably in order to avoid using God's name, Matthew generally uses the phrase 'kingdom of heaven' (31 times),

using 'kingdom of God' 4 times. In Luke, it is used 32 times and in Mark, 14 times.

7. Mark 1: 1–15
8. Mark 4: 10–12; 13: 1–36
9. 2 Kings 23: 10; Jeremiah 7: 31–32; 19: 5–6; 39: 35; Joshua 15: 8; 18: 16
10. 4 Kings 23: 10
11. 1 Enoch 27: 2; 90: 24–26; Ezra 7: 36; Mishnah, tractate Aboth 1: 5; 5: 19–20
12. E. Lohse, *Theological Dictionary of the New Testament*, Eerdmans, 1974, Vol.9, pp.424–437
13. Genesis 18: 4; Deuteronomy 28: 65
14. Exodus 3: 5; 29: 20; Joshua 10: 24
15. K. Dahn, *Dictionary of New Testament Theology*, Paternoster, 1978, Vol.3, pp.511–518
16. Mark 9: 35
17. Mark 9: 22, 43, 48–49
18. Luke 12: 49; 1 Peter 1: 7; 4: 12; Revelation 3: 18. See also Isaiah 48: 10
19. The *Advertiser* (Adelaide), March 17, 1987, p.25
20. Mishnah, tractate Gittin 9.10
21. Josephus, *The Life*, 426
22. Mishnah, tractate Gittin 9.3–5
23. Josephus, *Against Apion*, 2.201
24. Babylonian Talmud, tractate Gittin 57a
25. Mark 4: 10–12; 7: 17–23; 9: 28–29; 10: 23–31
26. *Aramaic Papyri of the Fifth Century BC*, A. Cowley (ed.), Oxford University Press, *No. 9, p.15*
27. Babylonian Talmud, tractate Gittin 57a. See also *Damascus Document*, 13.17; Mishnah tractates, Nedarim 11.12 and Arakin 5.6.
28. A. Oepke in *Theological Dictionary of the New Testament*, Vol.5, pp.639–643
29. J. Jeremias, *Infant baptism in the First Four Centuries*, SCM,

1960, p.49; O. Cullmann, *Baptism in the New Testament*, SCM, 1950, pp.25f., 71ff.

30. Justin, Martyr, *Apology* 1.61.4
31. D. Daube, *The New Testament and Rabbinic Judaism*, Athlone, 1956, pp.224–246
32. Further see G.R. Beasley-Murray, *Baptism in the New Testament*, Eerdmans, 1962, pp.320–329.
33. Compare E. Best, *Disciples and Discipleship*, T.&T. Clark, 1986, pp.93–94
34. See Matthew 18: 3.
35. Best, *op.cit.*, p.96

Chapter 7

1. Babylonian Talmud, tractate Taan 24b
2. See, e.g. Proverbs 12: 2; 13: 22; 14: 14; Ecclesiastes 9: 2.
3. See, e.g. 1 Chronicles 16: 34; Psalm 18: 1.
4. See, e.g., Genesis 15: 7–8; Psalm 37.
5. Saint Ambrose, *De Fide*, 2.1
6. Mark 1: 18, 20; 2: 14
7. Mark 5: 19–20
8. E. Schweizer, *The Good News According to Mark*, SPCK, 1971, pp.212–213
9. *The Age* (Melbourne), May 26, 1986, p.26
10. *The Weekend Australian*, November 19–20, 1988, 'Weekend', p.2
11. Mark 10: 25. Also see J. Duncan, M. Derrett, 'A Camel Through the Eye of a Needle', *New Testament Studies*, 32, 1986, pp.465–470.
12. Mark 10: 24, 26
13. Job 1: 3, 10
14. Deuteronomy 15: 7–11
15. Mark 1: 1, 14–15; 8: 35; 10: 29; 13: 10; 14: 9
16. See D.E. Nineham, *Saint Mark*, Penguin, 1969, p.276. See also 1 Corinthians 7: 12–14.

17. See 1 Corinthians 9: 5.
18. Compare Mark 11: 25.

Chapter 8

1. Compare Mark 3: 22.
2. See Mark 15: 40–51.
3. Compare Mark 10: 45.
4. Mark 16: 7; compare 14: 28.
5. Matthew uses *idou* 62 times, Luke 56, John 4 and Mark 7 times (1: 2; 3: 22; 4: 3; 10: 28, 33; 13: 23; 14: 41, 42).
6. Mark 14: 28; 16: 7
7. See, e.g., Matthew 7: 7–11; Mark 4: 24–25.
8. Compare Mark 8: 31.
9. See Mark 10: 42; 11: 17; 13: 8, 10.
10. Isaiah 50: 6; 53: 3, 7
11. Isaiah 53: 11
12. *The Martydom of St Polycarp*, 14
13. Isaiah 51: 17; Jeremiah 25: 15-38; see also Psalms of Solomon 8: 14–15; 1QaHab 11: 10–15; The Martyrdom of Isaiah 5: 13; Targum to Deuteronomy 32: 1.
14. Psalm 42: 7; 69: 2, 15; 124: 4–5; Isaiah 43: 2
15. John Lightfoot, *A Commentary on the Talmud and Hebraica*, Vol.2, 1658, Baker House reprint, p.269
16. Romans 6: 3–8. See also J. Duncan, M. Derrett, 'Christ's Second Baptism (Luke 12: 50; Mark 10: 38–40)', *Expository Times* Vol. 100, 1989, pp.294–295.
17. Acts 12: 2
18. Revelation 1: 9
19. *Interpreter's Dictionary of the Bible*, Abingdon, Vol.3, p.431
20. See 2 Maccabees 5: 1–27.
21. 1 Corinthians 9: 19
22. Mark 1: 38; see also 4: 21
23. See 1 Maccabees 2: 50; 6: 44; Thucydides, *History of the*

Peloponnesian War 2: 43.2.

24. Exodus 21: 30; Leviticus 19: 20; Isaiah 45: 13; also A. Deissmann, *Light from the Ancient East*, Hodder and Stoughton, 1910, pp.331–332

25. See, e.g., Romans 5: 15; J. Jeremias, *Theological Dictionary of the New Testament*, Vol. 6, p.536.

26. Compare Titus 2: 14.

27. See R. Marcus, '*Mebagger* and *Rabbin* in the Manual of Discipline vi, 11–13', *Journal of Biblical Literature* 75 (1965) pp.298-302; J. Jeremias, *Theological Dictionary of the New Testament*, Vol.6, pp.538–540.

Chapter 9

1. Steve Turner, *The King of Twist*, Spire, 1992, 'Disciples', p.31

2. Exodus 23: 8; Leviticus 21: 18; Deuteronomy 16: 19; Isaiah 6: 10; 29: 9–10; 1QSa 2: 5–7; 1QM 7: 4–5; Mishnah Peah 8: 9

3. See, e.g., Leviticus 19: 14; Deuteronomy 27: 18; 28: 29; 2 Samuel 5: 6–10; Isaiah 59: 10

4. W. Schrage, *Theological Dictionary of the New Testament*, Vol.8, pp.270–294

5. See, e.g., *The Testament of Solomon*.

6. See, e.g., 2 Maccabees 2: 7; 7: 29; 8: 27; Psalms of Solomon 14: 6; Sirach 5: 6; 16: 11-12; Wisdom 6: 6; 11: 9.

7. E.g., *Sophia of Jesus Christ*, 125–126

8. See further E. Lohse, *Colossians and Philemon*, Fortress, 1971, pp. 141–142.

9. See an example in Eusebius of Caesarea, *The History of the Church*, 6: 19.

10. The NRSV word 'again' is not in the Greek text.

11. See Mark 13: 11 and Michael G. Steinhauser, 'The Bartimaeus Narrative (Mark 10: 46–52)', *New Testament Studies* 32, 1986, pp.583-595.

Bibliography

Useful commentaries on Mark

Hugh Anderson, *The Gospel of Mark*, Marshall,
Morgan and Scott, 1976
Brings the text of Mark alive through offering many
details which set each passage in its first century context.

R. Alan Cole, *Mark*, IVP and Eerdmans, 1989
A practical, workaday commentary for those engaged in
Christian service.

Robert A. Guelich, *Mark 1–8: 26*, Word, 1989
This detailed, up-to-date, verse-by-verse commentary
deals with the state of the Greek text and modern scholar-
ly debate — as well as giving clear exposition of the
meaning of the Gospel passages and the book's ongoing
relevance.

John Hargreaves, *A Guide to St Mark's Gospel*, SPCK,
1965
A reference book for students, teachers or preachers wanting
to study the background of the Gospel and its message for
today as well as its use for their daily prayers.

Morna D. Hooker, *The Gospel According to St Mark*, Black, 1991

A detailed commentary on the author's English translation of Mark, focussing on the message of Mark to his readers.

Bas van Iersel, *Reading Mark*, T.& T. Clark, 1989

Employing the most recent methods of literary criticism, the writer helps the reader understand the main lines of Mark's story.

William L. Lane, *The Gospel of Mark*, Marshall, Morgan and Scott, 1974

The author has sought to concentrate on Mark's distinctive voice and has made extensive use of Roman, Greek and Jewish sources.

Eduard Schweizer, *The Good News According to Mark*, SPCK, 1971

Using the *Good News Bible* translation, this easily read book gives an introduction, a detailed exegesis and comments on the theology of each passage.

Vincent Taylor, *The Gospel According to St Mark*, Macmillan, 1966

Contains a wealth of valuable detail on the Greek text.

Useful general studies on Mark

Ernest Best, *Mark: The Gospel as Story*, T. & T. Clark, 1983

Deals with the Gospel as a whole, concentrating on key issues relating to Mark's theology — the unity of the Gospel, whether or not it was written for Christians or as an evangelistic document and what literary influences shaped the book.

Howard C. Kee, *Community of the New Age: Studies in Mark's Gospel*, SCM, 1977

The social setting and theology of the community to which Mark was writing are explored.

Jack Dean Kingsbury, *Conflict in Mark: Jesus, Authorities, Disciples*, Fortress, 1989

Focussing on the conflict Jesus has with various characters, the author explores the plot of the Gospel in order to elucidate Mark's explanation of the nature of Jesus and true discipleship.

Ralph P. Martin, *Mark: Evangelist and Theologian*, Paternoster, 1972

Includes discussions on the theology, Christology and various themes associated with the contemporary study of Mark.

Frank J. Matera, *What are they saying about Mark?*, Paulist, 1987

An easy-to-read summary of the most important recent Markan scholarship on Christology, discipleship and the origin, purpose and nature of the Gospel.

David Rhoads and Donald Michie, *Mark as Story: An Introduction to the Narrative of a Gospel*, Fortress, 1982

A study of Mark's narrative, settings, plots and characters.

Useful studies on discipleship in Mark

Ernest Best, *Disciples and Discipleship: Studies in the Gospel According to Mark*, T. & T. Clark, 1980

These essays, focussing on the central section of Mark, examine the role of the disciples and the impact of the disciples and discipling on the Twelve, on Peter, and on the family of Jesus.

Ernest Best, *Following Jesus: Discipleship in the Gospel of Mark*, JSOT, 1981

The purpose of this study is to enquire what discipleship meant in Mark's eyes — that is, 'What has Mark to say to the Christians for whom he writes about the nature of their Christian lives?'

Dennis M. Sweetland, *Our Journey with Jesus: Discipleship According to Mark*, M. Glazier, 1987

A detailed discussion of the major passages on discipleship to answer the question, 'What does it mean to be a disciple of Jesus Christ?'

Graham H. Twelftree, 'Discipleship in Mark's Gospel' in *St Mark's Review*, 141, 1990, pp.5-11

An article highlighting the contemporary significance of the chief characteristics of discipleship in this Gospel.

Useful studies on discipleship in the twentieth century

Dietrich Bonhoeffer, *The Cost of Discipleship*, SCM, 1959

A modern classic by a theologian who was martyred by the Nazis in 1945.

Dietrich Bonhoeffer, *Life Together*, SCM, 1954

A consideration of the directions and precepts the scriptures provide for Christians to live together.

David Watson, *Discipleship*, Hodder and Stoughton, 1981

A popular book on the various aspects of the challenge of living as a Christian in the twentieth century.

John White, *The Cost of Commitment*, IVP, 1976

An easy-to-read view of what it means to be a follower of Jesus today.

Useful treatments of present-day faith and life issues raised in Mark
❏ *Christology*

Jack Dean Kingsbury, *The Christology of Mark's Gospel*, Fortress, 1983

A comprehensive literary study of Mark's portrait of Jesus, setting out the meaning and function of the major titles of majesty applied to Jesus.

❏ *Ethics*

Dan O. Via, *The Ethics of Mark's Gospel: In the Middle of Time*, Fortress, 1985

The main section of this book deals with the ethical material in Mark 10.

William Barclay, *Ethics in a Permissive Society*, Collins/Fontana, 1971

Deals with the issues of work, pleasure, money and community.

❏ *Faith*

Christopher D. Marshall, *Faith as a Theme in Mark's Narrative*, Cambridge University Press, 1989

The author discusses the call to faith, the place of miracles in faith, faith and powerlessness, faith and discipleship, and the nature of unbelief.

❏ *The kingdom of God*

R.T. France, *Divine Government: God's Kingship in the Gospel of Mark*, SPCK, 1990

Discusses the meaning of 'the kingdom of God' for Mark's readers in the first and twentieth centuries.

❏ *Marriage and Divorce*

Wolfgang Schrage, *The Ethics of the New Testament*, T. & T. Clark, 1988

A comprehensive study which clarifies the ethical concerns of Jesus and the New Testament writers as well as examining concrete issues.

❏ *The Messianic Secret*

The Messianic Secret, Christopher Tuckett (ed.), SPCK and Fortress, 1983

A collection of nine essays on various aspects of this theme.

❑ Miracles, Healing and Exorcism

Reginald H. Fuller, *Interpreting the Miracles*, SCM, 1963
An introduction to the Gospel miracle stories.

Graham H. Twelftree, *Christ Triumphant: Exorcism Then and Now*, Hodder and Stoughton, 1985
Examines the practice of exorcism in Mark and other New Testament writings and explores their contemporary relevance.

❑ Wealth and Materialism

Jacques Ellul, *Power and Money*, Marshall Pickering, 1984
A challenge to reshape attitudes and lifestyles according to a biblical perspective, or forfeit all possibilities of being salt and light in the world.

Richard Foster, *Money, Sex and Power*, Hodder and Stoughton, 1987
Proposes principles for living a Christian life that are appropriate for modern society and authentically biblical.

Ronald J. Sider, *Rich Christians in an Age of Hunger*, Hodder and Stoughton, 1977
A searching call to affluent Christians to live a lifestyle nearer the Master they follow.

John V. Taylor, *Enough is Enough*, SCM, 1975
The subject of this book is excess — our consumption of food, our wage claims, our waste and pollution.